THE CULT OF iPOD

LEANDER KAHNEY

NO STARCH
PRESS

Printed in Canada

1 2 3 4 5 6 7 8 9 10—08 07 06 05

No Starch Press and the No Starch Press logo are registered trademarks of No Starch Press, Inc. Other product and company names mentioned herein may be the trademarks of their respective owners. Rather than use a trademark symbol with every occurrence of a trademarked name, we are using the names only in an editorial fashion and to the benefit of the trademark owner, with no intention of infringement of the trademark.

Publisher: William Pollock
Production Manager: Susan Berge
Cover and Interior Design and Composition: Octopod Studios
Developmental Editor: Patricia Witkin
Copyeditor: Pat Coleman
Proofreader: Stephanie Provines
Indexer: Ted Laux
For information on book distributors or translations, please contact No Starch Press, Inc. directly:

No Starch Press, Inc.
555 De Haro Street, Suite 250, San Francisco, CA 94107
phone: 415.863.9900; fax: 415.863.9950; info@nostarch.com; http://www.nostarch.com

Library of Congress Cataloging-in-Publication Data

Kahney, Leander.
    The cult of iPod / Leander Kahney.
        p. cm.
    ISBN 1-59327-066-6
 1. iPod (Digital music player) 2. Computers--Social aspects. I. Title.
    ML74.4.I48K34 2005
    006.5--dc22
                                        2005023404

THE CULT OF iPOD

iKahneys.

DEDICATION

To my wife, Traci, and our four beautiful kids: Nadine, Milo, Olin, and Lyle

ACKNOWLEDGMENTS

Thanks to the iPod community and everyone who shared a story, picture, or quote.

Thanks also to Phillip Torrone, Nobuyuki Hiyashi, Dennis Lloyd, and my colleagues at Wired News, especially Alison Macondray and David Miller. Also thanks to Patricia Witkin and Bill Pollock at No Starch Press.

Source

 TABLE OF CONTENTS

"MUSIC iS WELL SAID TO BE THE SPEECH OF ANGELS."

THOMAS CARLYLE

THE JOY OF iPOD: iCANDY FOR THE EARS

Fire, the wheel, and the iPod. In the history of invention, gadgets don't come more iconic than Apple's digital music player. The iPod is to the 21st century what the big band was to the '20s, the radio to the '40s, or the jukebox to the '50s—the signature technology that defines the musical culture of the era. And what a marvelous technology the iPod is. Inside Apple's little white box is magic, pure magic, in the guise of music.

Like a cell phone or a laptop, the iPod is kept close and carried everywhere. It's used every day, but not for work or to enslave you by persistent contact. The iPod is used to invoke euphoria. People are in love with music. The sparkling genius of the iPod is that it gives it to you in huge doses. The iPod can store an entire lifetime's worth of music. And so it becomes the most personal of personal devices. More than a computer, a car, or a fancy pair of shoes, it's part of your makeup, your personality. What's on it—the music—tells who you are. Music is deep in your heart and soul.

I'm a music junkie from England, a nation of music junkies. Since late childhood, music has been a passion, sometimes an obsession, that often took precedence over all other interests—food, love, even cigarettes. Like a lot of people, I had a giant collection of vinyl LPs and CDs that grew over the years into an unmanageable archive weighing hundreds of pounds. Too heavy for shelves, the records sat on the floor, spilling into the room. But for the most part, the collection was merely for other people to gawk at. I didn't play most of the records, and except for a few disks at the front of the pile, I forgot and neglected most of them.

Fast forward, and now the entire collection can fit inside a small white box the size and weight of a pack of cards. This to me is a miracle. A crowning achievement of technology. That unwieldy pile of vinyl and cardboard has been freed from the living room and is available anywhere and everywhere I go: from the earliest, regrettable singles to my latest obsession.

Inside the iPod, a music collection comes alive. There's delight in loading up a ton of stuff from all genres, eras, and styles and seeing what the machine comes up with. Select Random Shuffle, and the iPod dredges up tunes you might never consciously choose to play. But chosen for you, they're a delight. This mode of play also allows you to discover gems in a collection that previously sat unplayed on a shelf of CDs. Songs previously neglected can become top favorites. And then there are all those tunes you never knew you had. Random shuffle can create great surprises, selecting just the right song at just the right time. Or it can throw together unexpected combinations: Burning Spear followed by Ludacris. It doesn't always work, but when it does, you're in pop heaven.

The iPod has changed forever my listening habits. No longer do I want to hear an album all the way through (with rare exceptions). What I want is a playlist of my favorites. Listening to the iPod makes a cinematic adventure of a trip to the supermarket or a boring car drive. It adds a sense of otherworldliness to walking down the most familiar street. There's nothing better for exercise—pounding beats and breaks to get you energized to mount the summit of a hill. I like listening to the iPod while riding my bike (yeah, I know its dangerous and probably illegal). High as a kite off the exercise, the music transports me to nirvana. Sometimes, when the right tune pops up, I'm truly in heaven.

The magic of the iPod is the music it contains.

THE 10,000 HIT WONDER

The iPod is a bona fide hit—a genuine cultural phenomenon. Everyone has one, from your kid sister to the president of the United States. It's beloved of glue-sniffing skate punks and observant Jews who load it with thousands of niggunim, or humming songs. The word iPod is already a proprietary eponym (such as Kleenex or Xerox) for all MP3 players: the word iPod denotes them all.

The iPod is changing the music industry—not just how music is played and enjoyed, but how it is distributed and, maybe soon, how it is made. The iPod has usurped the album as the key product of the music industry, replacing it with the playlist. When it comes to digital music, playlists are the way to organize, listen to, and discover new music. The playlist is king.

The iPod has rescued and redefined Apple. The computer company may yet turn into a music company or one that sells all kinds of entertainment devices. Apple already sells more iPods than computers. Apple was the right company in the right place at the right time. Thanks to Napster and other file-sharing software, hundreds of millions of people suddenly had huge music collections on their computers.

In the late '90s, at the height of Napster's power, it was easier to download songs than to rip them from a CD. After all, it was often less bother to search online than hunt down the CD on your shelf. As well as downloading contemporary stuff, people re-amassed their entire record collections—everything they owned on unplayed stacks of LPs, CDs, and cassettes.

But all this digital music was tied to the computer. Burning CDs of downloaded music is a headache. The natural solution is to copy it from hard drive to hard drive. Apple took the tiny Japanese hard drives just coming onto the market, slapped a nifty interface on them, and provided a fast connection to suck music from the computer.

Apple has a no-compromise approach to products. It usually makes them as well as it can, no matter the cost, and this has been an advantage, not an impediment. The iPod was beautifully conceived and executed. It was marketed expertly and became a word-of-mouth hit. The media, chatter on the Internet, and the white headphones catapulted the iPod into everyone's pocket and backpack.

The iPod is dead easy to use. Pick it up, and in 30 seconds you've mastered the basics. But it goes deeper. The iPod is beautifully integrated with the computer, which feeds it tunes, and with an online store to fill it at 99 cents a pop. The iPod is amazingly versatile. You can listen to it while driving—through the car stereo—or use it as an alarm clock to wake you in the morning. It's not only a personal stereo, it's the home stereo, the office stereo, or the stereo at the gym. It's both personal and public, used by DJs, and in bars and hotels. It's even starting to take over some nightclubs. The iPod has created DJs out of mere mortals. A host of new clubs encourage patrons to spin tunes off their iPods for others to dance to—if they don't get booed off.

And the iPod has spawned all kinds of new businesses—from services that load iPods for people with more money than time, to song stylists who create playlists for surgeons to operate to, to those who compile playlists for newborns fresh out of the hospital nursery.

The combination of hardware, software—and music—proved to be a hit. Apple took it to Windows, and the rest is history.

iPOD CULTURE CLUB

This book examines the birth of the iPod, its meteoric rise to fame, and the culture that has grown up around it. It details some of the fun things people do with their digital players and the homage they pay it.

CHAPTER 1 describes the iPod's inauspicious introduction by Steve Jobs, who called it a "breakthrough device," but no one believed him at the time.

CHAPTER 2 introduces the iPod's unacknowledged father, Tony Fadell, who sold Apple on the idea of a digital player tied to an online music store. Before going to Apple, Fadell tried to interest Sony, who turned him away.

CHAPTER 3 looks at our new listening habits, the revelatory joys of shuffle play, and how letting people peek at your music collection can ruin your image or encourage someone to sleep with you.

CHAPTER 4 is about the iPod's runaway word of mouth, the emergence of homemade iPod ads, and celebrity users such as the fashion designer who owns 70 iPods and a gilded-carrying case to lug them around in.

CHAPTER 5 examines iPod culture. It describes MP3Js and software thieves who use iPods to steal expensive applications from computer stores. It also takes a look at people who dress up as iPods for Halloween.

CHAPTER 6 looks at iPod homages from fans: the thousands of snaps of iPods in famous places; the fantastic future devices fans design to show their wishes and desires; and iPod culture in New York as revealed by online personal ads.

CHAPTER 7 is about iPodtrepreneurs, or iPod entrepreneurs, and the booming business of accessorizing the iPod. It looks at the rise of iPod scams and swindles and how to get a free iPod off the Net.

CHAPTER 8 wraps it up with a look at the cultural impact: how the iPod is changing social snobbery on college campuses, and its impact at Microsoft, where employees are so enthusiastic about the iPod, it's starting to upset Bill Gates.

The iPod Zone: Back in the '80s, Bauhaus front man Pete Murphy starred in an iconic ad for Maxell audiocassettes that had him weathering a speaker-powered typhoon to the strains of "Night on Bald Mountain." **CREDIT:** iLOUNGE

II Now Playing

1 of 8

iPods for
All

0:00   -2:40

MENU

LIVERPOOL JOHN MOORES UNIVERSITY
LEARNING SERVICES

UNVEILING A BREAKTHROUGH DEVICE

We were very lucky—we grew up in a generation where music was an incredibly intimate part of that generation. More intimate than it had been, and maybe more intimate than it is today, because today there's a lot of other alternatives. We didn't have video games to play. We didn't have personal computers. There's so many other things competing for kids' time now. But, nonetheless, music is really being reinvented in this digital age, and that is bringing it back into people's lives. It's a wonderful thing. And in our own small way, that's how we're working to make the world a better place."
—Steve Jobs in a Rolling Stone *interview, December 3, 2003.*

In mid-October 2001, Apple's publicity department sent out invitations to a media event at its shiny corporate headquarters in the heart of Silicon Valley. The event would mark "the unveiling of a breakthrough digital device," the invite read. Apple is notorious for withholding information about new products until they're released, and as usual, the invitation gave almost no information about what the event might herald. It gave the time and date—October 23 at 10AM—and nothing more. There was, however, a cryptic clue at the bottom:

"Hint: it's not a Mac."

Immediately, scores of news websites published articles about the invitation, sparking fevered speculation about what the "breakthrough device" might be. "Our forums, and the forums at every other Mac website, are experiencing record traffic," reported the Mac Observer. Most sites guessed Apple would unveil a portable music player, but in the absence of any real information, people's imaginations ran wild. Across the Web, people speculated that Apple would introduce a nifty handheld, something like a PalmPilot on steroids—a device capable of playing not just music, but movies too. And it would take photos, make phone calls, and mix cocktails....

This rampant speculation created such a magical aura around the mystery device, people said they were going to buy it sight unseen. "We have noted many people saying that they wanted this new device, without even knowing what it was," the Mac Observer said. Even professional industry watchers, such as technology industry analyst Rob Enderle, got caught up in the excitement. Enderle told "CBS Marketwatch" he was "75 percent sure the company had something more than a (music) player in mind."

On the morning of the 23rd, about 200 journalists, guests, and Apple staff gathered in a wood-paneled auditorium to see what charismatic Apple CEO Steve Jobs had up his sleeve. Dressed in his trademark black turtleneck and jeans, Jobs took the stage with a confident stride. "We have something really stunning for you today," he announced with a big grin. Jobs is in his element introducing new products for Apple. His presentations are the tech equivalent of a rock show or a good stand-up routine. They generate tremendous anticipation, even among jaded journalists who believe themselves immune to tech industry hype.

Though Jobs's presentations are generally straightforward, he throws in several jokes and makes great use of multimedia. He often shows new Apple TV ads or specially made promotional videos, always at ear-splitting volume. Jobs knows he's starring in his own infomercial, but he lends the proceedings an air of grown-up dignity and excitement. He's very charming and funny. He paces the stage, delivering utterly hyperbolic lines with a straight face; the Mac's being "insanely great" is his most famous.

He also knows how to pace a product launch. Things start slowly, with background facts about Apple's performance or the market in general. Jobs knows that everyone is waiting for the inevitable introduction of the next "insanely great" new product, and he builds suspense accordingly, usually waiting until the end of the presentation, just when he appears to be wrapping things up. Almost as an afterthought, Jobs will say there's "one more thing," and, with a mischievous grin, pull back the curtain.

On this particular October 23, Jobs began by recapping Apple's "digital hub" strategy. The Mac is the center of a digital lifestyle, he said, in which our lives are increasingly mediated by digital devices. Consumers use digital cameras and camcorders, they download movies and share pictures over the Net, and the computer is the core, or hub, of this experience. Jobs noted that Apple made its software to work with all kinds of digital cameras and camcorders, but as yet, no device had been made especially to work just with the software. Until now.

"The field we chose was music," Jobs said. "Why music? Well, we love music, and it's always good to do something you love." Jobs went on to explain that music is a part of everyone's life. "It's a large target market," he said. "It knows no boundaries. And there is no market leader. No one has really found the recipe yet for digital music. And not only will we find the recipe; we think the Apple brand is great for this."

Jobs discussed other portable digital music players on the market, running through all the options: flash-memory players, hard drive players, CD players, and CD-MP3 players. Then he got to the punch line. Holding up a little white box about the size of a pack of cards, Jobs said that Apple was introducing its own hard-drive based music player: iPod. "I think this blows them away," he said.

Jobs described how iPod could store songs in a variety of formats and how it represented three breakthroughs: One, it's "ultra-portable"; two, it's "ultra-thin"; and three, its 5 GB internal hard drive can hold 1,000 songs. "To have your whole music library with you at all times is a quantum leap when it comes to music," Jobs said. "And iPod fits in your pocket. Never before possible."

Jobs then spent the next 20 minutes going through the iPod's features, including 20-minute skip protection and a superfast FireWire connection. An entire CD could be downloaded in 5 to 10 seconds, he said, and the iPod's battery could be recharged in one hour. Jobs demonstrated the "unique" scroll wheel and how the iPod automatically synchronizes itself with iTunes jukebox software. "Isn't this cool?" enthused Jobs, showing how the iPod automatically downloads new songs when plugged into a computer. "It's

never been this fast or this easy before," he continued. "We've all heard 'plug and play' before. This is plug, unplug, and play." Jobs added: "There's been nothing like this before. And I don't think there's another company that could do this. To bring everything under one roof together to be able to create a product like this."

Jobs said the iPod would cost $399 and be available November 10, 2001. It would be, he predicted, "the hottest gift this holiday season." Jobs dimmed the lights to show a promo video featuring company executives and pop stars, including Moby and Seal, who'd gotten an early peek at the machine. "Do you remember what it was like when you got your first Walkman?" said Seal. "Wow! I want to carry this wherever I go."

"You've got your own record store in this thing," said Steve Harwell, the lead singer of Smashmouth. "This kicks every other product's ass right here."

Jobs concluded the event with a hint that Apple might introduce a version for Windows. "We have thought that when we get a little spare time, we will look at taking it to Windows," Jobs said. "We know the experience won't be as good, but we will probably look at that down the road."

BREAKTHROUGH, MY EYE

Though Steve Jobs called the iPod a "breakthrough" device, few people agreed with him at the time. Several digital music players based on hard drives were already on the market. The first was introduced two years earlier, in October 1999, by Compaq. Created by the company's research labs, the Personal Jukebox, or PJB, was designed around a 6.5 GB hard drive. But the PJB was as big and ugly as a brick, and it didn't sell well.

A French company, Archos Technology, had better luck with the Archos Jukebox. Resembling a diminutive Wurlitzer jukebox in blue and silver plastic, the Archos had already gone through two versions and could record MP3 files as well as play them.

Another popular player came from the Singapore company Creative, whose Nomad Jukebox had also been through a couple of versions. The latest model, at 20 GB, had four times the iPod's capacity. And it sold for the same price: $399.

So when Apple came along with the iPod, it was neither the first hard drive player, nor the biggest, nor the cheapest. And, of course, it only worked with Macintosh computers. Few people saw anything breakthrough about it. Indeed, the initial reaction was overwhelmingly negative. "The iPod sells for an absolutely hideously outrageous $399 and will be available to the two people who buy them at that price on November 10," said the MacSlash website in a news piece reporting the iPod's introduction earlier that day. On the site's forums, one poster wrote, "Apple has introduced a product that's neither revolutionary nor

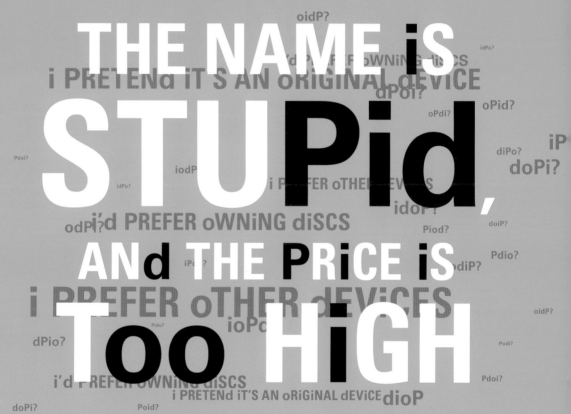

THE NAME iS STUPid, ANd THE PRiCE iS Too HiGH

—BRYAN CHAFFiN

THE iPod RANKS AS ONE OF THE GREATEST CONSUMER ELECTRONICS SCORES OF ALL TIME

—BUSINESS 2.0

breakthrough, and they've priced it so high that it's reminiscent of the Cube." The Cube was Apple's elegant but expensive cubic computer from 2000. It won critical praise but sold poorly. The author went on to offer some ideas for what the letters in "iPod" stood for. "Idiots Price Our Devices," the poster suggested, or "I Pretend it's an Original Device." Others chimed in: "I'd Prefer Owning Discs," said one, and "I Prefer Other Devices."

Some people liked iPod from the start, of course ("Impressive Piece of Design," wrote one), but surprisingly, most people were indifferent at best. Some were even outraged. Writing for *Wired News*, MacCommunist columnist Lukas Hauser, said "smash the iPod." "Apple had been claiming we were going to be treated to a 'breakthrough' device with the iPod's release. But the only 'breakthrough' here is a growing desire to break a 2-by-4 over Steve Jobs' skull," Hauser wrote. "iPod. iYawn," wrote the popular Mac columnist Rodney O. Lain on the Mac Observer site.

"The name is stupid, and the price is too high," added the site's editor, Bryan Chaffin.

TWEAKS AND SALES

But four years later, Steve Jobs has been proven right. His hyperbole was justified. The iPod *is* a breakthrough device—a technology that, thanks to its size, ease of use, and ability to store a lifetime's worth of music, is transforming the music industry.

As of April 2005, Apple had sold more than 10 million iPods. By comparison, Sony sold only 3 million Walkmans in its first three years. The iPod commands an astonishing 92.7 percent of the market for hard-drive players, according to sales and marketing information company the NPD Group. Some analysts expect the market for digital music players to grow exponentially in the next few years, from about 10 million units in 2002 to 100 million units in 2006. By 2010, there'll be 500 million digital music players—one for every 15th person on the planet—according to estimates published by *Business 2.0* magazine.

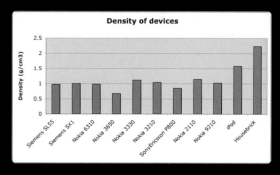

Density of devices

Weapon of Choice: iPod Mini

Of all the uses for the iPod, here's one of the most unexpected: defensive street weapon. Phil Leif, a designer from Washington, DC, successfully defended himself during a street robbery with an iPod. And it wasn't even a full-sized iPod; the attack was foiled with an iPod mini.

Here's what happened. One Saturday evening, just as it was getting dark, 19-year-old Leif was walking through a sketchy part of the nation's capital. As he headed for his Metro stop, Leif fished out his iPod mini to change songs. Suddenly, he felt someone grab his shoulder from behind. Having been the victim of a bag-snatching just the week before, Leif was jumpy about another street robbery. He spun around and smashed the guy with the base of his iPod mini. "It connected pretty hard with his forehead," Leif said. "I felt a very strong connection between my hand and his head. There was a good 'aaargh' and he grabbed his forehead. I kicked him in the stomach. He doubled up and I ran away."

(ABOVE) It's no wonder the iPod makes a good weapon. The iPod is nearly as dense as a house brick, according to calculations by Mobile Entropy. CREDIT: MOBILE ENTROPY; (BELOW) Phil Leif and his iPod mini, which he smashed into a mugger's forehead. CREDIT: PHIL LEIF

The iPod mini is an effective weapon, he said, especially when wielded like a down-turned knife. "It's solid metal," he said. "It's a sharp little thing." Leif described the potential robber as probably a homeless man with a "big dirty beard." Leif admitted that he may have been a little overzealous and might have attacked a harmless street person instead of a mugger. "If he was asking for a dollar or some help, I

feel horrible," he said. "But I can't really say." Leif's friend, Alex Payne, said the mugger was lucky Leif wasn't armed with the 40 GB iPod, which is a lot bulkier than the mini.

And while Apple's share must surely slip, the market for portable players is becoming truly vast. At present, Apple owns it. "The iPod ranks as one of the greatest consumer electronics scores of all time," declared *Business 2.0*.

In the last four years the iPod has changed. The biggest difference? It works with Windows PCs. Though the iPod has sold fairly well since its inception, it really took off when Apple fully embraced the world of Windows. But the stampede wasn't immediate when Apple introduced the first Windows-compatible iPod in July 2002. The real change occurred nearly a year later, when Apple enhanced the way the iPod connects to a computer. In May 2003, with the introduction of the third-generation iPod, Apple added USB 2 connectivity instead of just the standard FireWire. FireWire is common on the Mac, but relatively rare on the PC. USB 2, on the other hand, is becoming standard on Windows PCs and is just as fast.

Adding USB 2 was a subtle shift for Apple. It marked a departure from the principle of making products primarily for the Mac platform. But it also had the most dramatic impact on sales. Prior to the May 2003 switch, Apple had sold 1 million iPods. But within the next six months, it had sold another million iPods, and nearly 3 million more were sold within a year. In the next 18 months, 9 million more were sold.

Apple has also diversified the iPod to match every outfit and budget. It comes in all shapes and sizes, from the diminutive Shuffle to the multicolored Mini. More important, it hits just about every $50 price point between $100 and $600, ensuring there's an iPod for every pocketbook.

Like Paris Hilton, the basic white iPod is thinner and lighter than ever, and its capacity has jumped dramatically, from 5 GB to 60 GB (and will likely be 80 or 100 GB by the time you read this).

U2 has its own iPod, and there have been laser-etched, celebrity-signed iPods from the likes of Beck, Madonna, and No Doubt.

BUY TUNES

Part of the magic of the iPod is the software it connects to—iTunes—a program for organizing music, ripping CDs and playing Internet radio. And most important: for buying tunes off the Net.

Like the early iPod, the iTunes Music Store was Mac-only at first. It was introduced at a splashy launch event in downtown San Francisco in April 2003. The Windows version followed in October. To hear Steve Jobs tell it, the iTunes store is the beginning of the end for file-sharing networks. "This has been the birth of legal downloading," Jobs declared at the launch event. "We're going to fight illegal downloading by competing with it. We're not going to sue it. We're not going to ignore it. We're going to compete with it."

According to Jobs, competing with file-sharing networks means providing things such as reliable, one-click downloading, good-quality sound, and liberal usage rights. Plus, buying songs from Apple is legal. No one is going to be sued by the Recording Industry Association of America for doing it. "It's good karma," Jobs said. "You're supporting artists. You're not stealing." "The Apple online music store is going to be the hottest way, we think, to acquire digital music," he told the crowd of 200 press members, musicians, and executives from the music and computer industries. Clad again in his usual jeans and turtleneck and looking fashionably stubbly, Jobs explained how the service strikes the right balance between the convenience of downloading music over the Net and the need for the industry to get paid. The service, he said, allows Apple to refashion its controversial mantra from a couple of years ago, "Rip, mix, burn," into the much more music industry friendly "Acquire, manage and listen."

Built into iTunes (and already dubbed "Buy Tunes" by wags), the service was hailed by musicians, analysts, and executives as a breakthrough (yes, another one!) in online music distribution. "It's not free, but it's 99 cents a song, pretty doggone close," Jobs said. "There's no legal alternative that's worth beans."

"It's great news for the whole industry," said Dennis Mudd, CEO of Musicmatch, who attended the event. "It's the first pay-music service that's better than illegal music services." (Musicmatch partnered with Apple to provide the software for the first Windows version of the iPod.)

In October, at the launch of the Windows version of the iTunes store, Jobs again called on his friends in the music business to pitch the new service. Patched in from Dublin by videoconference, U2's Bono said the new service was a "really, really cool thing." "That's why I'm here to kiss the corporate ass," said Bono, drawing a huge laugh and applause from the crowd. "I don't do that for everyone."

"Thank you so much," said Jobs sarcastically.

Speaking from London by videoconference, Mick Jagger said it was a shame digital downloading of music had gotten off to a bad start with courtroom battles and illegal file-sharing services. He said he hoped initiatives such as the iTunes Music Store would be successful. "Hopefully it can go forward and be something everyone is happy with," he said.

Right from the start, the music store was a big hit. The Windows version attracted a million users in its first three days, and by early 2005, the store accounted for more than 70 percent of all music sold online, according to Apple.

According to Apple, the best customer at the iTunes store has spent a cool $29,500 on music. Steve Jobs joked that the customer's parents haven't seen their credit card bills yet.

Copy Protection or Business Protection?

All the songs purchased through the iTunes Music Store are copy protected by a scheme called FairPlay. Prior to the online store, the iPod didn't support copy-protection technology.

Most pundits would tell you that the music industry pushed the addition of copy protection to shield its music from online file sharing. But as technology journalist Ian Betteridge has pointed out, Apple's not necessarily worried about piracy. The iTunes FairPlay system has another purpose: it locks songs to the iPod. Without it, songs bought at the iTunes store could be played on any portable player, and the lack of a tie-in would be a threat to Apple's nicely sealed, three-part system.

WHY IT WORKS

In the late 1990s, Apple was in big trouble. Its competitors in the PC industry were selling ever-cheaper commodity PCs, and Apple—the only company that made both the hardware and software—started looking like a dinosaur. Unlike Microsoft, Apple hadn't successfully licensed its technology to other companies, and it insisted on controlling the whole widget—from the system software to the one-button mouse. Critics said Apple's proprietary technology was too expensive and incompatible with the rest of the world. As sales plummeted, the company seemed destined for the boneyard. But Apple scraped by, thanks to a string of popular products such as the iMac.

And now, with the iPod, the qualities that appeared to spell Apple's early doom, such as the rigid control over hardware and software, have become its best assets. By exercising control over the hardware and the software, Apple has been able to construct the easiest-to-use digital music system possible. Unlike the glitch-prone systems of its competitors, Apple's three-way combination of hardware (iPod), software (iTunes), and online service (music store) is about as seamless as a sophisticated tech product gets. As Steve Jobs told *Rolling Stone*:

Apple has a core set of talents, and those talents are… very good hardware design… very good industrial design; and we write very good system and application software. And we're really good at packaging that all together into a product. We're the only people left in the computer industry that do that. And we're really the only people in the consumer-electronics industry that go deep in software in consumer products. So those talents can be used to make personal computers, and they can also be used to make things like iPods. And we're doing both, and we'll find out what the future holds.

Randall Stross, a Silicon Valley author and historian, wrote that Apple's combination is "an ingeniously conceived blend of hardware, software and content that made buying and playing music ridiculously easy." Compare this with Sony, which, until early 2005, sold a selection of digital music players that couldn't play MP3 files. This is because Sony owns one of the world's big four record labels, Sony BMG Music Entertainment, which includes Arista, Columbia, Epic, and RCA, among others. Sony saw the MP3 format as a threat to its music business, and so it crippled its own players by restricting them to its proprietary compression format, known as Atrac, even though the MP3 format is the de facto standard for digital music. Trouble is, Atrac files won't play on portable players made by other companies, and Sony's players wouldn't play files downloaded from other companies' online stores. As a result, Sony's digital players have not found a customer base, and only in 2005 did the Japanese giant finally throw in the towel on Atrac and wholly embrace the ubiquitous MP3 format. It may be too little, too late though.

SIZE

THICKNESS

COST

Dan Turek lives in a small town where all the radio stations are either bad or don't come in clearly. Turek listens to his iPod during his morning commute. Trouble is, the commute is only 20 minutes. By the time Turek tunes his iTrip FM transmitter, scrolls through all the songs, adjusts the volume, and retunes the iTrip, he's parking in the office lot. On the way home, more often than not, he'd see an empty battery icon blinking on the iPod's screen.

"Then one morning it hit me, why not pop in that Morrissey cassette that had been sliding around the floor mats for the past six months?" Turek said. "Voilà — instant music. I had forgotten how easy it could be. I was now able listen to an entire side of a cassette on my commute instead of my usual one and a half songs." Plus, it sounded better. "I had crystal clear, rich, analog sound. So one morning I did my first comparison test since my fourth grade science project (which carpet cleaner works best). I compared everything I could think of between the iPod and cassette, and an hour later the results showed a clear winner.... My results seem to have had little effect, as the iPod continues to sell through the stratosphere."

| CAPACITY | DURABILITY | THE RESULT |

Playboy's iBod is a service for downloading explicit pix to the iPod photo. In 2004, *Playboy* offered six galleries of assorted pictures, including Playmates, Blondes, and Voluptuous Vixens — but only to paying members of its Cyber Club.

"If iPod photo is 'a feast for the eyes' on its own, it's a veritable ocular orgy now that Playboy.com has dialed up the heat a few notches," the company said.

Did Apple deliberately sabotage the iPod photo to make it useless for storing porn? Tokyo-based blogger Keith Finch thinks so. Shortly after buying one of the devices, Finch noticed that his iPod photo occasionally introduced pictures from other albums while viewing a slide show. Finch initially thought it an annoying but meaningless bug. Then he wondered what might happen if an iPod photo owner stored saucy pictures in "private" albums, not intended for public consumption. "Just imagine," Finch wrote in e-mail, "you're click-click-clicking along, and ... suddenly WHOA!, without warning or explanation an unthinkable image from your double-secret 'Hot Butts' photo album appears!" Finch continued: "Perhaps some right-thinking person on the iPod photo firmware team inserted this 'bug' on purpose, as a feature to help discourage sinfully minded types from loading up their iPods with porn."

(ABOVE) In New York, some people think the iPod's white earbuds are "showy."
CREDIT: CAESAR LIMA

Now Playing

2 of 8

New Listening Habits

0:00   -2:56

MENU

Downloading copyrighted songs from file-sharing networks may be illegal, but it sure is great for building a music library. At their peak, file-sharing networks such as Napster and its short-lived successor Audio Galaxy were the ultimate in wish fulfillment. Think of a song, any song, and it was instantly available—for FREE. At times, it seemed as though the world's entire catalog of recorded music were available, even if, in reality, it was only a portion of the modern, Western canon—the Backstreet Boys, mostly.

The file-sharing networks almost achieved what has been called the Celestial Jukebox: a networked library of all the music ever recorded, available instantly, anywhere, any time. Though still a ways off, Apple's online iTunes store aspires to this. Imagine all the music ever made—from Gregorian chants to techno made just for a sneaker ad. And each song can be bought with a single click, high quality guaranteed. With unlimited virtual shelf space, an online music store can stock anything and everything. It matters not if a particular track sells a million times a week or once in a millennium. A sale is a sale—and revenue from the accumulated sales of obscure tracks can equal, if not better, sales of the hits.

At present, the iPod is a good approximation of the Celestial Jukebox. If you've ripped all your CDs and download new music, you can have an entire lifetime's worth of music on the iPod. Playing it can be like listening to an amazingly comprehensive personal radio station, but one that plays only the good stuff.

MUSIC MAGIC FOUND IN THE SHUFFLE

Napster revolutionized music distribution, but massive libraries of digital music and capacious players such as the iPod are upending listening habits through something very simple but profound: random shuffle. When music lovers first discover the iPod or software such as iTunes, they often rhapsodize about the joys of randomly shuffling tracks. "I have seen the future, and it is called Shuffle," wrote Alex Ross, the *New Yorker*'s music critic, after he acquired an iPod.

Stuffy old listening habits—such as playing albums from beginning to end—are being thrown out in favor of allowing machines to choose songs at random, which often leads to unexpected, and magical, juxtapositions of music. "There is something thrilling about setting the player on Shuffle and letting it decide what to play next," Ross wrote. "The little machine often goes crashing through barriers of style in ways that change how I listen."

Random shuffle is nothing new. It first became popular as a feature of CD players. But with CDs, shuffling tracks is typically limited to the songs on a limited number of disks. Randomly selecting tracks really comes into its own with giant music collections: libraries that stretch to tens of thousands of songs. In a giant library, random shuffle is a good way—sometimes the only way—to play music that would otherwise go unheard. With the explosive growth of file sharing and CD ripping, supersized personal music libraries aren't even the exception but the norm. During a discussion on the Web of ways to manage ever-growing music collections, one contributor noted his library stretches to 120 GB. Another counted the number of songs in his library that he'd never actually heard: 20,000.

(ABOVE) Lecturer Michael Bull says the iPod is the perfect way to manage your experience. (See his interview on page 25.) He says music is the most powerful medium for thought, mood, and movement control. CREDIT: iLOUNGE; (FACING PAGE) CREDIT: JOY OF TECH

Lecturer Michael Bull, an expert on the social impact of personal stereos, said random shuffle can turn large music libraries into an "Aladdin's cave" of aural surprises. Bull, a lecturer in media and culture at the University of Sussex in the United Kingdom, interviewed hundreds of iPod users for a study. He reports one of his interviewees as saying, "I tend to listen to the iPod on random a great deal of the time.... With a large music collection, it is very easy to forget some of the gems that are in there, and random tends to bring some of those out again." Bull said, "Their music collection becomes a treasure trove full of hidden delights which the magic of the machine throws up at them. Some users feel that the machine intuitively understands them by giving them just the type of music they want to listen to when they want it."

As columnist Steve Bowbrick noted in *The Guardian*, "This is a radically different way of encountering music and one I don't need to tell you is not possible in any other format."

Bull concurred. Bull said random shuffle has become one of the key components of new listening habits ushered in by digital music. "Most users say they use (random shuffle) sometimes," Bull said. "Some—about 25 percent—use it most of the time. It's an important component of listening."

KELLARIS JOKED

Apple picked up on this phenomenon and exploited it with the iPod shuffle, a smaller, cheaper iPod that dispensed with a screen in favor of allowing the player simply to play a selection of tunes at random. Increasingly, bloggers are celebrating the joys of random shuffle by posting lists of Random 25 tracks thrown up by their digital jukeboxes, as a search of Google attests.

James Kellaris, a professor of marketing at the University of Cincinnati and author of a study about tunes that stick in your head, said the appeal of random shuffle is likely generational. Kellaris joked that random shuffle likely appeals to the MTV generation—kids with short attention spans who are likely "brain damaged." "The feature should appeal to variety seekers with a low need for control," he said. "Random shuffle is a control freak's worst nightmare." Kellaris said he wondered if random shuffle is having a deleterious long-term effect on listeners' attention spans. "Personally, and I believe I speak for many old farts here, I appreciate listening to music, be it an opera or a pop album, in the sequence in which the artist decided to present it," he said. "Temporal order is an important element of how a work unfolds dynamically over time, an important factor underlying the aesthetic effect. Random shuffle pretty much flushes that down the toilet."

Bull noted that most listeners use random shuffle in particular settings or in certain moods. Sometimes, he said, people can't decide what to listen to, a problem easily solved by random shuffle.

Although people often create playlists for specific activities (walking, driving, commuting, working out, and so on), they also enjoy giving control to the machine, which can surprise and delight with unexpected selections of tracks, Bull said. The player will sometimes put together combinations the user would never have dreamed of. One user interviewed by Bull, for example, said the iPod "colors" one's surroundings, and random shuffle can significantly change one's perceptions of a familiar place.

"As it's on shuffle, I don't know what's coming up next, and it often surprises me how the same street can look lively and busy and colorful one moment, and then, when a different song starts, it can change to a mysterious and unnerving place," Bull reports the interviewee as saying. "I like the sensation though."

Bull said the random selection of tracks allows the user to create unique personal narratives, such as a private movie soundtrack, or to bring up surprising memories. "There's elements of *The Dice Man* here, coupled with the power to listen to things in a unique way—a sequence that will probably never be repeated—that makes their music collection even more exciting and mysterious," he said.

LIKELY APPEALS TO

ATT E

LIKELY "BRAIN DAMAGED."

Random shuffle is an important component of the digital music experience. Apple recognized this with the iPod shuffle, which can simply play a selection of tunes at random. **CREDIT:** iLOUNGE

THAT RANDOM SHUFFLE

Discussing the joys of random shuffle, the *New Yorker's* Alex Ross wrote: "I've transferred about a thousand songs, works, and sonic events from my CD collection to my computer and on to the MP3 player. There is something thrilling about setting the player on Shuffle and letting it decide what to play next. Sometimes its choices are a touch delirious — I had to veto an attempt to forge a link between György Kurtág and Oasis — but the little machine often goes crashing through barriers of style in ways that change how I listen. For example, it recently made a segue fvrom the furious crescendo of "The Dance of the Earth," ending Part I of "The Rite of Spring," right into the hot jam of Louis Armstrong's "West End Blues." The first became a gigantic upbeat to the other. For a second, I felt that I was at some madly fashionable party at Carl Van Vechten's. On the iPod, music is freed from all fatuous self-definitions and delusions of significance. There are no record jackets depicting bombastic Alpine scenes or celebrity conductors with a family resemblance to Rudolf Hess. Instead, music is music."

Party at Carl Van Vechten's

THE MTV GENERATION — KIDS WITH SHORT ...ION SPANS WHO ARE

Jon Carroll, a columnist with the *San Francisco Chronicle*, discovered the downside to random shuffle on a road trip. In addition to a lot of music, Carroll had loaded his iPod with an audio book of Dostoyevsky's *The Brothers Karamazov*. He wrote: "It was not until Pennsylvania that we realized that we had neglected to turn off the 'random' feature of the iPod, so we were getting chapters in arbitrary order, the plot entirely in the mischievous hands of fate. We loved the part at the beginning, where everybody died."

The Perils of Random

iPod Shuffle in Three Steps

When Apple introduced the iPod shuffle, it tried to spin its lack of a screen into a positive feature by emphasizing the ability to listen to songs at random. Unimpressed, Mark Husson, a software developer from Denver, Colorado, posted instructions on the Web showing how to turn any iPod into an iPod shuffle in three easy steps:

1.

Get a Post-it Note

2.

Get your iPod

3.

Put the Post-it Note on the iPod

"Now you can enjoy the iPod shuffle's cool new feature without having to go buy a new player. Enjoy!" he wrote.

(BELOW RIGHT) The iPod has taken the place of record sleeves of old, according to Bull. In the old days, record covers provided an aesthetic for music. With digital music, the aesthetic has left the record and is now in the player: the iPod. **CREDIT:** iLOUNGE; **(BELOW LEFT)** No Bull: Lecturer Michael Bull is known as "Professor iPod" for his expertise in the societal impact of personal music devices. **CREDIT:** MICHAEL BULL

25

BULL SESSION WITH PROFESSOR iPOD

Michael Bull is "the world's leading—perhaps only—expert on the social impact of personal stereo devices," according to *the New York Times*.

Bull, a lecturer in media and culture at the University of Sussex in the United Kingdom, is the author of *Sounding Out the City: Personal Stereos and the Management of Everyday Life* (Berg Publishers, 2000), a book Bull calls the "definitive treatment" of the impact of the Sony Walkman and its descendants. Now Bull has turned his attention to Apple's iPod.

Bull interviewed hundreds of iPod owners about how, when, where, and why they use the iPod and how it integrates into their everyday lives.

The interviews are the basis for Bull's recent book, *Sound Moves; iPod Culture and Urban Experience*. The book, due to be published in late 2005, examines the impact of cell phones and car sound systems, as well as iPods.

I interviewed Bull for Wired News just after Apple released the iPod mini.

WIRED NEWS: What do you make of the iPod mini?

MICHAEL BULL: The iPod mini will be popular. Sales will expand as the market expands. It's a repeat of what happened with the Walkman 25 years ago. Apple is out front of a massively expanding market. Their machines are brilliant in every respect....

At the moment, they can't lose, but Apple will eventually lose its dominant market share. The competition will be too intense.

One of the interesting things is that with vinyl, the aesthetic was in the cover of the record. You had the sleeve, the artwork, the liner notes. With the rise of digital, the aesthetic has left the object—the record sleeve—and now the aesthetic is in the artifact: the iPod, not the music. The aesthetic has moved from the disc to what you play it on ... and the iPod mini will appeal to those who want an artifact for style....

The other thing is that there's a lot of illegal downloading. Half the people I've talked to so far download music illegally. The investment they're making is going into the artifact, not the music. The market is moving toward the artifact, not the music to fill it.

Bull noted that a lot of users reported they stored a few "perennial favorites" on their iPod but generally were constantly shuffling new music in and out, which may explain why they're reluctant to pay for something they don't "keep."

WN: Apple has always said the iTunes Music Store was a loss leader, a way to sell more iPods.

BULL: Right. In terms of usage, Apple got it intuitively right. People use [the iPod] as an alarm clock, and when they listen to it at night, they like the fact it can turn itself off. It's how people like to use music. I don't think Apple did much research into how people would use their players, but they got most of it right. For example, a lot of people use it to go to work, for commuting. I found that they use the same music on a regular basis. They will often play the same half-dozen tunes for three months, and each part of the journey has its own tune....

It gives them control of the journey, the timing of the journey, and the space they are moving through. It's a generalization, but the main use [of the iPod] is control. People like to be in control. They are controlling their space, their time, and their interaction ... and they're having a good time. That can't be understated—it gives them a lot of pleasure.

So, for example, music allows people to use their eyes when they're listening in public. I call it non-reciprocal looking. Listening to music lets you look at someone but don't look at them when they look back. The earplugs tell them you're otherwise engaged. It's a great urban strategy for controlling interaction.

It's also very cinematic. The music allows you to construct narratives about what's going on. Or you use it to control thoughts. A lot of people don't like to be alone with their thoughts. The best way to avoid that is to listen to music.

A lot of people don't like where they're going in the day. If you can delay thinking about that until the last minute ... People don't take off their earplugs until the very last minute, until they're inside the door at work. It's a great way to control mood and equilibrium.

WN: What about listening habits? How have personal stereos changed the way people enjoy music?

BULL: It gives people totally private worlds. Before the Walkman, people never thought that they could take music with them and control their listening environments. But personal stereos reflect a cultural drift. There's a long history of individualized listening—kids with stereos in their bedrooms, for example. In the '20s people listened to radios with headphones....

The Walkman, and now the iPod, is the perfect mobile acoustic environment. It's better than listening to the stereo in a car....

But it's not just about creating a private acoustic environment. Walkmans were used sometimes to share music. Walkmans used to come with two headphone jacks.

I think music has become more personal.... For the people I interviewed, the music on their portable stereos was different from the music they listened to at home. The music often reminded them of something nice. It was very personal. They don't want others listening to it.

It fits in with general cultural trends—doing things when you want to do them. With the iPod, you have your music when you want it. It controls your interaction with people and places on your terms.

WN: But does it make people antisocial? Is music less of a social experience than it used to be? *the New York Times* ran an article last week about New Yorkers using their iPods to block out the city. But isn't that the point of personal stereos? What's different about the iPod that wasn't true of the Walkman?

BULL: People like to control their environment, and the iPod is the perfect way to manage your experience. Music is the most powerful medium for thought, mood, and movement control.... the *New York Times* asked what becomes of the public space when the public space becomes privatized. What about the others—the person in the supermarket checkout you don't recognize is there? It asks whether the public space becomes colder as the personal space becomes warmer through music.

There's a lot of studies in the literature that demonstrate with the urban space, the more it's inhabited, the safer you feel. You feel safe if you can feel people there, but you don't want to interact with them.

Music allows people to find pleasure in the place where they're existing. [Personal stereos] make the user's life much better. It helps them manage urban life.... Urban life is one of the reasons they're using these devices. How often do you talk to people in public anyway?

(BELOW) BULL: The iPod is a good way to control public space. It makes the mundane cinematic and allows people to control their thoughts and mood on the way to work, for example. **CREDIT**: iLOUNGE

27

(ABOVE) Bull thinks the iPod is linked all the way back to radios of the '20s: just another way to make listening personal. **CREDIT**: iLOUNGE

28

PodBrix : 1000 Brix

UNIT
LIMITED

Tomi's Tiny iPod People

A PodBrix Minifig in the hand is worth two on eBay. Originally sold for $17, the limited edition figures have commanded more than $200 on eBay. **CREDIT:** TOMI

Tomi's 300 PodBrix Minifigs before they were shipped to customers. **CREDIT:** TOMI

OF 300

N . 300 UNITS

An artist called Tomi has created a mini business from selling mini iPod LEGO figures and T-shirts. In February 2005, Tomi introduced his first product: a limited run of silhouette iPod people made from little LEGO figures colored black. Resembling the iPod ads that inspired them, each "PodBrix Minifigs" figure was mounted on a monochrome background and numbered and signed on the back. Limited to a run of 300 units, the $17 figures sold out in a matter of hours. "All 300 units sold out in less than 10 hours, and frankly, I didn't imagine that kind of response," said Tomi by email.

Shortly afterward, to mark Steve Jobs's 50th birthday, Tomi created a LEGO version of the Apple CEO delivering a keynote speech. The limited edition LEGO Jobs is portrayed onstage clutching an iPod and an iPod shuffle. His image is projected on a backdrop behind him—just like a real Macworld Expo keynote. Again, the figure was limited to 300. It went on sale at midnight (ET) February 25, 2005, for $17 and sold out in 36 minutes.

The next day, several of the figures showed up on eBay. Many sold for $200 or more for a couple of weeks, before the craze died down and the figures returned to more reasonable prices.

In March 2005, Tomi introduced the "Brixwear 1000" T-shirt. Sporting a picture of a silhouette Minifig, the shirt has a small magnet behind the figure's hand, allowing an iPod shuffle to be "stuck" to the shirt as though the LEGO figure were holding it. The shirts, which were limited to a run of 300, sold out in 18 minutes.

PodBrix
1000 brix in your pocket

The **Joy of Tech**™   by Nitrozac & Snaggy

©2005 Geek Culture®

Steve Jobs' playlist:

She's so high
Beautiful Day
The Tide is High
Rocket Man
Pulled Up
Up, Up and Away
Up!
I'm a Believer
Take My Breath Away
Top of the World
Fly Me to the Moon
We Are The Champions

joyoftech.com

Theme song for Apple stock: *Vertigo*

3

II Now Playing

3 of 8

A Star Is Born: The Making of the iPod

0:00   -2:38

MENU

Tony Fadell sold Apple on the idea of an MP3 player linked to an online music store, according to Ben Knauss, who worked with Fadell to bring the iPod to life. "This is the project that's going to remold Apple, and 10 years from now, it's going to be a music business, not a computer business," Fadell predicted in early 2001. CREDIT: DOC SEARLS

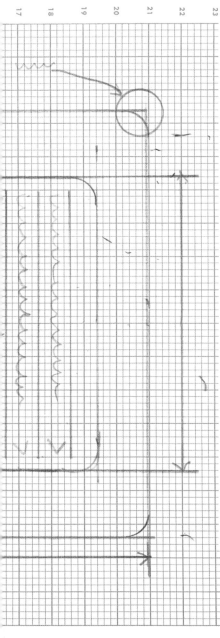

One of the weirdest open secrets in Silicon Valley is that engineer Tony Fadell is the unacknowledged father of the iPod. The general impression, promoted by Apple, is that CEO Steve Jobs and Apple's head designer, British-born Jonathan Ives, created the iPod between them. Though Apple has never made this claim directly, it's a myth the company's PR department is happy to perpetuate. In an early promotional video, for example, Ives talked about the process of creating the iPod, giving the impression he and his team had designed it themselves.

But though Ives and Jobs made massive contributions, the iPod appears to be the brainchild of Tony Fadell, a 36-year-old computer engineer with an impressive career creating consumer electronic devices. I say "appears" because, under Jobs, no one at Apple except a few top executives is permitted to talk to the press. Even then, conversations are strictly "on message," and questions about who designed what are off limits. Fadell himself is forbidden from talking and has turned down several requests for interviews.

For several years, however, Fadell has been telling his story at conferences and campus recruiting fairs, and lots of tantalizing tidbits are also spread across the Web. Take his bio at the Strategic News Service, which was likely written by Fadell himself.

"Tony Fadell is ... responsible for creating the first two generations of Apple's new iPod digital music device," the profile says. "After researching and designing the iPod product solution as a contractor in eight weeks, he was hired to create the implementation team."

Fadell may not be talking, but others are, including Ben Knauss, a former senior manager at PortalPlayer, the company Fadell approached to help develop the iPod. A privately held startup, Portal-Player had come up with "reference designs," essentially schematics, for several digital music devices, including a small portable player.

Knauss acted as the primary liaison between Apple and Portal-Player during the device's development. He quit the company in late 2001, just before the iPod came to market—a move that earned him an online moniker, the iClod. According to Knauss, the iPod originated with a business idea dreamed up by Fadell. "Tony's idea was to take an MP3 player, build a Napster music sale service to complement it, and build a company around it," Knauss said. "Tony had the business idea."

Fadell graduated from the University of Michigan in the early 1990s with a degree in computer engineering. He worked at General Magic, an Apple spin-off, and Philips Electronics, where he helped develop handheld PDAs. He also worked briefly at RealNetworks when it was developing its online music service, Rhapsody, according to the *New York Times*. In the late 1990s, Fadell quit Philips to launch his own company, Fuse, to develop and sell a range of gadgets, including a digital music player. But Fadell failed to attract funding, according to the *Times*, and so started shopping his idea around Silicon Valley. No one, including Sony, was interested—except Apple.

In February 2001, Fadell started working at Apple as an independent contractor designing the iPod and planning the company's audio strategy, according to Fadell's resume, which is available online. He must have done something right. Within two months, in April 2001, Apple named Fadell the head of its iPod and Special Projects group. In a few short months, his 30-member team of designers, programmers, and hardware engineers had assembled the iPod largely from off-the-shelf parts or technologies licensed from other companies.

Knauss said at one of the first meetings with PortalPlayer, Fadell declared, "This is the project that's going to remold Apple, and 10 years from now, it's going to be a music business, not a computer business."

"Tony had an idea for a business process, and Apple is transforming itself on his whim and an idea he had a few years ago," Knauss added.

Knauss also recalled that Fadell always dressed in matching clothes and accessories, and every day in a different color. "One day it would be purple, the next lime green," Knauss said. "His shirt, pants, shoes, socks, cell phone cover, key fob, even the rims of his glasses; every single part of him would be the same color when he came in for a meeting." One might wonder if it's mere coincidence that the iPod mini comes in a rainbow's worth of colors too.

Knauss said Fadell was familiar with PortalPlayer's reference designs for a couple of MP3 players, including one about the size of a pack of cigarettes. And though the design was unfinished, several prototypes had been built. "It was fairly ugly," Knauss said. "It looked like an FM radio with a bunch of buttons." The interface, he said, "was typical of an interface done by hardware guys." But Knauss said Fadell recognized the design's potential. "Tony figured the product was there." "[PortalPlayer] was attractive to Apple because we had an operating system," said Knauss. "That was a real selling point for Apple. We had the software and the hardware already done, and Apple was on a tight schedule." Knauss said the reference design was about 80 percent complete when Apple came calling. For example, the prototype wouldn't support playlists longer than 10 songs at that point. "Most of the time [Apple spent] building the iPod was spent finishing our product," Knauss said.

At the time, PortalPlayer had 12 customers designing MP3 players based on the company's reference design. Most were Asian hardware manufacturers, Knauss said, but also included were Teac and IBM. Big Blue planned a small, black MP3 player, based on the company's own mini hard drives, which featured a unique circular screen and wireless Bluetooth headphones. "The design for IBM was a lot sexier," Knauss said.

An iPod prototype. To prevent competitors seeing what Apple was working on, prototypes were housed in a shoe-box–sized enclosure, with the controls, screen, and jacks on the outside. To prevent Apple suing us, we made this illustration from a spy photograph sneaked out of Apple's design lab. CREDIT: BRIAN BEHNKE

Sony's iPod

If things had gone differently, Sony might have developed the iPod instead of Apple, a well-placed source claims. In the late 1990s, PortalPlayer was also working on an iPod-like music player for Sony, said a source who works for Sony in Tokyo and who asked to remain anonymous. "PortalPlayer was working with Aiwa, a subsidiary of Sony," the source said. "Aiwa was so close to finishing the product, but Sony killed it. I saw the prototype. It was one of the coolest MP3 players I have ever seen." "The executives at Sony regret that decision," the source said.

"[THE iPOD] IS THE PROJECT THAT'S GOING TO REMOLD APPLE, AND 10 YEARS FROM NOW, IT'S GOING TO BE A MUSIC BUSINESS, NOT A COMPUTER BUSINESS."

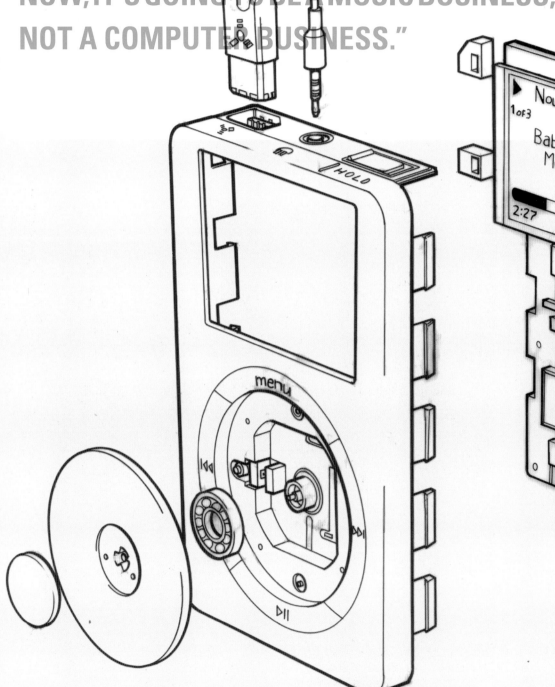

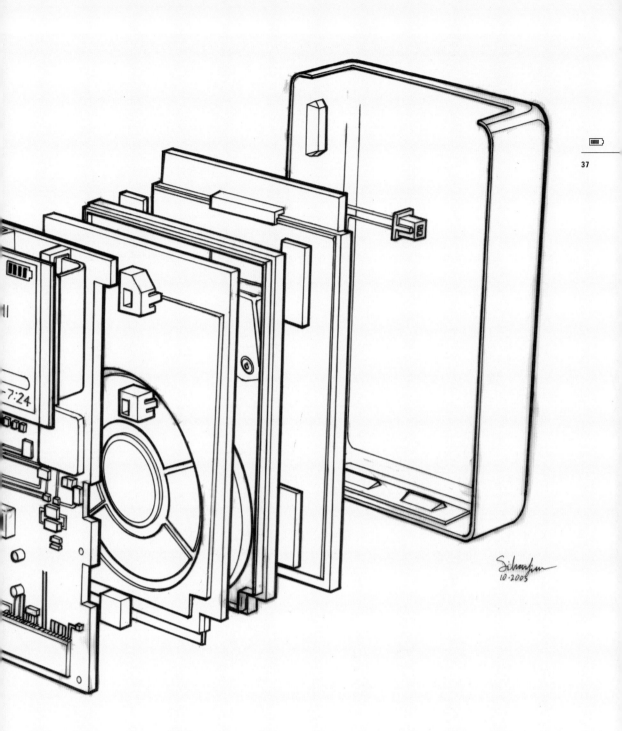

The original iPod was assembled from a host of off-the-shelf parts: a Toshiba hard drive, a battery from Sony and key chips from Texas Instruments and Sharp. Even the basic hardware design was licensed from a small Silicon Valley startup company, PortalPlayer. CREDIT: SILVAN LINN

But PortalPlayer went exclusively with Apple. "When Apple came to the table, we dropped all our other customers," Knauss said. For the next eight months, the company's 200 employees in the United States and 80 engineers in India worked exclusively on the iPod, Knauss said.

Apple had a list of features it wanted added to the reference design: Apple's preferred music format, AAC, as well as Audible's audio book format, and a five-band equalizer. Apple also wanted a new interface, which it designed in-house in about three months, Knauss said.

And although Fadell may have had the business plan, Apple CEO Steve Jobs molded the device's design and interface. "The interesting thing about the iPod is that since it started, it had 100 percent of Steve Jobs's time," said Knauss. "Not many projects get that. He was heavily involved in every single aspect of the project." At the beginning of the project, Jobs held meetings about the iPod every two to three weeks, but when the first iPod prototypes were built, Jobs became involved daily. "They'd have meetings, and Steve would be horribly offended if he couldn't get to the song he wanted in less than three pushes of a button," Knauss said. "We'd get orders: 'Steve doesn't think it's loud enough, the sharps aren't sharp enough, or the menu's not coming up fast enough.' Every day there were comments from Steve saying where it needed to be." Knauss said Jobs's influence was sometimes idiosyncratic. For example, the iPod is louder than most MP3 players because Jobs is partly deaf, he said. "They drove the sound up so he could hear it," Knauss said.

Knauss noted that there were no demands to add FairPlay, Apple's copy-protection technology. It was appended later to the second-generation iPod to coincide with the introduction of the iTunes Music Store. "There was no discussion of [digital rights management]," Knauss said. "Their belief was DRM would hurt sales when they rolled out the music store. They specifically wanted no DRM in the original iPod."

Knauss said all the iPod prototypes—and there were several—were sealed tightly inside a reinforced plastic box about the size of a shoe box. "They put the buttons and the screen in creative locations all over the box so people couldn't tell what product was inside it and how small it was," Knauss said. "They always put the controls in different places—the scroll wheel on the side, the screen on the top—to make sure it wasn't predictable what the end design was. The only thing accessible was the jacks."

Knauss said the iPod project was nearly killed just as it drew to completion. Tests showed the iPod drained its batteries even when powered down. "It would have run three hours before going dead, and that was when it was turned off," Knauss said. "The production lines had already been set up," Knauss said. "That was a tense part of the project. For eight weeks they thought they had a three-hour MP3 player." Knauss said the problem was eventually fixed, and shortly afterward, Apple bought a majority stake in the company.

Knauss stayed on until near the end of the iPod's development but quit shortly before it was released because he had no confidence it would be a success. "It was probably a mistake, but then you have to go with what you think at the time," he said. Knauss, 33, is now contracting for Microsoft.

Apple, IBM, and PortalPlayer did not respond to requests for comment, though PortalPlayer confirmed Knauss had been employed as a senior manager.

NOTE: *After* Wired News *published this story in July 2004, PortalPlayer threatened a lawsuit unless the story was taken down. PortalPlayer threatened* Wired News *with misappropriation of trade secrets, and on the advice of our lawyers, we ignored them. There was a flurry of faxes for a couple of days, and then nothing. Because the story was no longer on the front page, perhaps PortalPlayer thought it had been withdrawn. Maybe the company simply dropped the matter. We never did find out.*

that supplied the digital-to-analog converter for turning MP3 files into sound.

It may sound like assembling LEGO bricks, but a device of the iPod's complexity is not easily put together. The hardware suppliers praised the feat: the iPod was compact and light and produced phenomenal sound. "The value is putting it all together and optimizing the design to eke out the best performance, get the best power utilization, the best audio performance," Julian Hayes, vice president of marketing at Wolfson, told Electronics Design Chain. "That is not a trivial task by any means. Sometimes it's very difficult in a cost constrained [situation] and small form factor to get the performance."

The first-generation iPod is about the size of a pack of cards and just a little heavier. It has a white Perspex (a type of Acrylic) top with a small square screen and a circular "scroll wheel" mounted on ball-bearing bushings. The scroll wheel has a push button in the middle, and, together, they form the entire interface.

The back of the first iPod is shiny stainless steel. It sports an Apple logo and, often, a personal inscription. Apple offered laser engraving for $50 initially and later for free. Unlike competing portable players, the iPod has no openings at all: no battery compartments or slots for extra memory or other peripheral add-ons. It's as tightly wrapped as a nut. To crack the case, a screwdriver or similar tool has to be jimmied between the back metal plate and the Perspex front, before carefully prizing the two pieces apart.

Inside, the internal components are sandwiched together compactly—there's almost no air space. On top is the battery, a flat silvery package that is almost as long as the iPod itself. The battery lies on top of the hard drive, which is also slim. The hard drive is attached by tape to the main motherboard. Beneath the motherboard lie the scroll wheel and the small, square, monochrome screen.

THE HARDWARE

Tony Fadell and his design team started work on the iPod in the spring of 2001. It was assembled from bits and pieces of hardware and software developed by other companies—something highly unusual for Apple—but the company added its own magic: excellent industrial design and a simple, intuitive interface. Apple brought the device to market in about eight months.

According to a 2002 article in Electronics Design Chain, most of the internal electronics—including the main circuit board—were developed by PortalPlayer. A hardware design company, PortalPlayer had developed a reference design that could be used to make a variety of digital audio products, from a portable digital music player to a full-sized stereo for the living room. Several of the devices could be made from standard, readily available parts but could also be easily customized. Apple reportedly chose PortalPlayer because of the high audio quality of its design.

"Choosing a development platform allowed Apple to focus on its true genius for form factors and user interfaces," wrote reporter Eric Sherman.

Most of the iPod's other components were also bought or licensed on the open market. The iPod's slim, rechargeable battery was purchased from Sony, its tiny, 1.8-inch hard drive from Toshiba. The drive is likely the most expensive component, accounting for about half the hardware costs. Other key bits and pieces were bought from Texas Instruments, Sharp Electronics, and Wolfson Microelectronics, a small Scottish company

THE SOFTWARE

The iPod's interface was initially based on software devised for cell phones by Pixo, another Silicon Valley startup. Although Apple designers conceived of the iPod's elegant interface—the hierarchical, scrollable menus of artists, songs, and genres—the underlying nuts and bolts were provided by Pixo, including low-level graphics, memory management, and database functions, according to the programming website of Amit Singh, an IBM researcher. In addition, Pixo provided applications such as the address book, calendar, and to-do list. A small, privately held company, Pixo was founded by a former Apple product manager, Paul Mercer, who had also worked on Apple's PDA, the Newton. The company was staffed by several ex-Apple engineers.

As Apple developed the iPod, it discovered the software was one of the trickiest parts. As the launch date approached, Apple's initial effort at an operating system wasn't nearly ready, according to reports. Thanks to their Apple contacts, Pixo staffers heard of the dilemma and offered to license their operating system and applications, which had been originally developed for cell phones. According to reports, the legal negotiations took longer than the actual programming. "We were able to get something running and demonstrate it in a couple of weeks," Mercer told the *San Francisco Chronicle*.

However, relations quickly soured. Within months of the iPod's launch, Pixo was complaining about the money it got from Apple, which wasn't enough to sustain the company. There were layoffs at Pixo, though some engineers who had worked on the iPod were subsequently hired by Apple, which now positions itself as being wholly responsible for developing the iPod's software. The rest of Pixo was sold to Sun Microsystems in June 2003.

Pixo's contribution was never formally announced. Apart from a few scattered reports, the only clue was mention of the company in the "About iPod" screen in early versions.

The iPod Killer: pPod

There's been a lot of talk of "iPod killers," competing players that will blow the iPod out of the market. But to date, none have come along, except perhaps for the pPod from a British software firm, StarBrite. StarBrite's pPod was a virtual iPod for Pocket PCs, a software iPod that ran on Pocket PCs, Microsoft's Palm-like operating system for handhelds.

The virtual iPod was, well, virtually identical to a real iPod. The application filled the Pocket PC's entire screen with a faithful facsimile of the iPod, including the player's distinctive scroll wheel and four buttons for playing, pausing, and so on. Like the iPod, the pPod was controlled by its virtual scroll wheel. Pocket PCs have touch-sensitive screens, which allow users to navigate the pPod's menus with their fingers—just like the iPod.

Naturally, the pPod's interface was also just like the iPod's. Songs were arranged by a series of nested menus, which could be browsed by artist, album, genre, and so on. Alas for StarBrite, Apple quickly shut it down. StarBrite pulled the software from sale, and it has not been heard from since.

Developed by the British software firm StarBrite, the pPod was a short-lived software iPod that ran on Pocket PCs, Microsoft's Palm-like operating system for handhelds. CREDIT: PHILLIP TORRONE

The **Joy of Tech**™ by Nitrozac & Snaggy

joyoftech.com

II   Now Playing   ▭▭▭

4 of 8

Spreading the Word
of iPod: Runaway
Word-of-Mouth

0:00   -3:42

MENU

FEW PRODUCTS HAVE CAUGHT THE PUBLIC'S ATTENTION IN THE SAME WAY AS THE iPOD

Apple is rightly regarded as one of the best-marketed companies in the world. Its brand is iconic, and its advertising is frequently awarded, imitated, and parodied. But for the iPod, the most powerful advertising came from unprecedented word of mouth, tons of media, and the lucky accident of using white earbuds.

Apple has spent relatively little money to promote the iPod. A big nationwide marketing campaign can cost $200 million a year or more, but Apple spent only $25 million to launch the iPod in 2001, and about $45 million in 2004, according to estimates by ad tracking firm TNS Media Intelligence. Most of that money was spent on the award-winning silhouette dancer TV campaign. The TV ads did their part, but the iPod was largely advertised by extensive word of mouth.

"The product was well marketed because Apple did not over-market it, especially when it became a runaway success," said Douglas Atkin, a New York ad man and author of *The Culting of Brands* (Portfolio, 2004). "They stepped back and let the consumers and the media take over—much more credible marketers."

Few products have caught the public's attention in the same way as the iPod. New users don't just like their iPods; rather, they become enthusiastic evangelists, telling everyone at every opportunity the joys of the device. What's on their iPod is a favorite topic among bloggers, and several people have made their own homebrew iPod ads in homage to the machine.

The media has also become iPod obsessed. The *New York Times*, for instance, doesn't let a week pass by without at least a couple of iPod

(FACING PAGE) Despite giant iPod billboards the world over—these are in Amsterdam—experts say the iPod wasn't overmarketed. CREDIT: BOYINUK/ SPYMAC; **(BELOW)** The white earbuds were a lucky marketing accident. Apple made the earbuds white to keep them consistent with the player, but they also served to advertise the player, even when it was hidden in a bag or pocket. CREDIT: iLOUNGE

stories. The iPod has made the cover of most major magazines and newspapers, and several publications run regular pieces on celebrities' iPod playlists. It's been featured on Oprah Winfrey's TV show and high-lighted in several music videos and movies.

And then there's the lucky accident of the white earbuds. On the street, the distinctive earbuds serve to advertise the player hidden in the wearer's pocket. "The white earplugs are a sort of Masonic handshake to other users that they've got the 'right' MP3 player—a subtle shared code," said Atkin. "It's immediately obvi-ous that it's not a Sony or any of the other pedestrian brands."

Coloring the earbuds white seems like a stroke of marketing genius, but it appears to have stemmed from a decision simply to keep the color consistent with the rest of the device. "I remember there was a discussion: 'Headphones can't be white; headphones are black or dark gray,'" Apple's head designer, Jonathan Ives, told the *New York Times*. According to the *Times*, "Uni-form whiteness seemed too important to the product to break the pattern, and indeed the white headphones have become a kind of secondary, unplanned icon."

Indeed, they are iconic. To Doug Holt, an Oxford University marketing professor and author of *How Brands Become Icons* (Harvard Business School Press, 2004), the iPod's success is due to fortuitous design decisions like that. "This is primarily a design story, including the buds," he said.

(ABOVE) Advertising the iPod at the Gare Montparnasse in Paris, France. **CREDIT**: MIKE SERIEYS; **(FACING PAGE)** The media has become iPod obsessed. The iPod is a regular fixture in magazines, newspapers, and TV shows. **CREDIT**: iLOUNGE

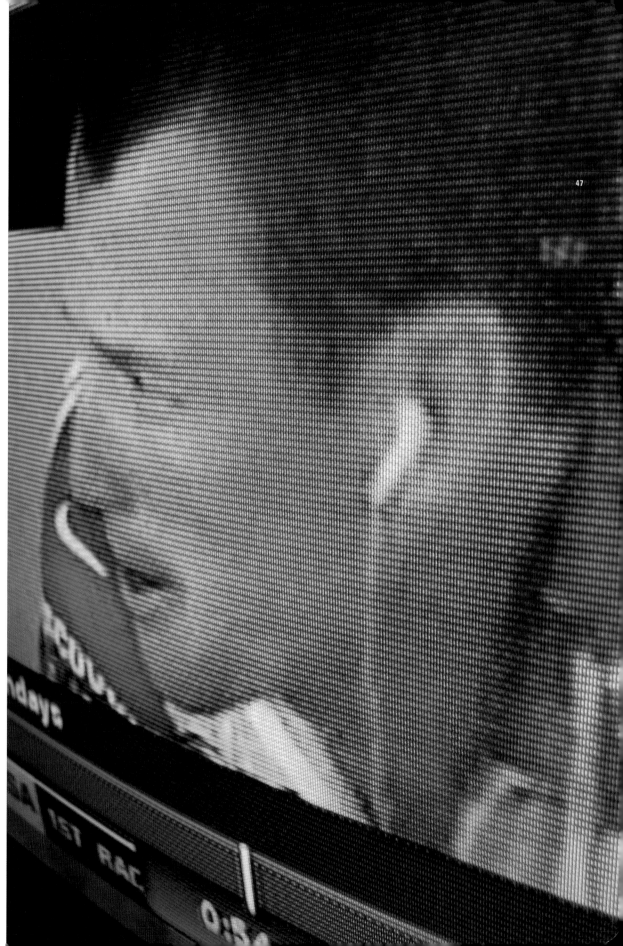

HOMEMADE ADS
COULD PLAY A BIG PART
IN MARKETING, JUST LIKE BLOGGING
IS SHAKING UP THE NEWS.

HOMEBREW iPOD ADS

In 2004, school teacher George Masters had the marketing world abuzz with a homemade iPod ad that rapidly went "viral." Masters's 60-second animated ad features flying iPods, pulsing hearts, and swirling '70s psychedelia. It's set to the beat of "Tiny Machine" by '80s pop band the Darling Buds.

Masters quietly posted the spot to his personal website in November 2004. It received moderate traffic until it was picked up by several blogs. In a matter of days, the ad had been watched more than 37,000 times and was making the rounds on blogs and email. The ad caught the attention of marketers, who praised its professional production values and proclaimed it one of the first "pure" advertisements seen on the Internet. Though homemade ads are nothing new, most are parodies, protests, or political commentaries. Masters's is pure advertising—its purpose is to promote the iPod and nothing more.

To some experts, Masters's ad heralded the future of advertising. Homemade ads could play a big part in marketing, just like blogging is shaking up the news. Gary Stein, an online advertising analyst with Jupiter Research, said he was struck by the quality of Masters's ad and its marketing savvy. "It shows great advertising principles," Stein said. "He's computer-literate, but he's also literate in the language of advertising.... You could take this thing and put it on MTV this afternoon. It's not only good, it's good advertising. People go to college to learn this. He just gets it." Stein said Masters's ad is the first "straight-up" consumer-produced spot of which he's aware. Stein said he's seen spec ads from agencies made to attract clients and viral ads created by pros disguised to look grassroots, but he had not seen a TV spot created by a fan. Though Masters's ad looks like it was done by a pro, he is actually a 36-year-old high-school teacher from Orange County, California. He created the spot in his spare time. Working a couple of hours at a stretch, the ad took five months to make. Itis part homage to Apple and the iPod and part portfolio builder, but mostly, Masters said, he just made it for practice. "I did it for fun," he said. "I love motion graphics. I like creating visuals."

Masters said he was inspired to make the ad while listening to the Darling Buds' song. The title, "Tiny Machine," reminded him of the iPod; the ad's style was inspired by pop videos from the '80s shown on cable music channel VH1. He posted the ad, he said, for comments and suggestions. And if anyone wants to hire him, he'll consider all offers. "I'm pretty much working in a vacuum here," he said. "You think, 'Is this good?' That's why I put this stuff out there, to get some feedback." He's received a lot of nice comments and some criticism, which he welcomes. "The critical comments are the most helpful," he said. "They help the review process."

Masters said he's quite aware the ad is nothing like Apple's campaigns featuring silhouette dancers. "It's off-brand, but that's the point," he said. "That's the fun of being one guy. You're not limited by a style guide or a creative director. You can branch out and think different."

Steve Rubel, a vice president at New York PR agency CooperKatz and author of the Micro Persuasion weblog, said evangelistic customers such as Masters will play an increasing role in marketing for companies. "It's a sign that consumers want to have a role in promoting a product they love," he said. "There's a real trend toward consumer-generated media. People are creating news, they're blogging. People will create marketing as well. This guy is a great example."

Another example Rubel cited is the ongoing Spread Firefox campaign, a collective promotion of Mozilla's web browser that included raising money to buy a big ad spread in the *New York Times*. Mozilla, however, was founded on the model of open source software, which encourages the computer programming community to contribute and collaborate on software development. So, Mozilla is no stranger to growing itself via grassroots communication.

Stories about customer evangelism abound, and word-of-mouth or "buzz" marketing is seen as an important and growing part of advertising. But TV spots are new territory. "It's customer evangelism," Rubel said. "It's not going to happen for every company, only those with a passion. The Mac platform, and the iPod, have created a core following, a customer passion. People want to spread the love." He added, "I hope [Masters] gets a job in Apple's marketing department. He certainly deserves it. But I'm surprised Apple hasn't shut it down. They can be very persnickety about their brand and trademarks."

Masters is not the only person to make free marketing materials for Apple. Global Mechanic, a Canadian multimedia production company, made an iPod TV ad on spec, and designer Daniel Oeffinger crafted one for a class at the Savannah College of Art and Design. Like Masters's ad, Oeffinger's spot featured swirling iPods and pulsing hearts. "Apple's brand definitely evokes these images, and I think it's cool that George tapped into them in a completely different way," said Oeffinger.

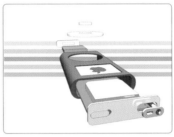

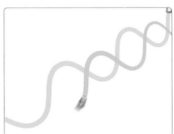
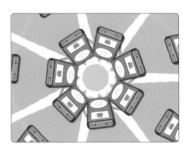

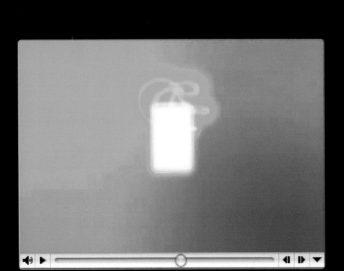

Designer Daniel Oeffinger also crafted an iPod for a college class. Like Masters's ad, Oeffinger's spot featured swirling iPods and pulsing hearts. "Apple's brand definitely evokes these images," Oeffinger said.
CREDIT: DANIEL OEFFINGER

Stills from George Masters's homebrew iPod ad, which features flying iPods, pulsing hearts, and swirling '70s psychedelia.
CREDIT: GEORGE MASTERS

51

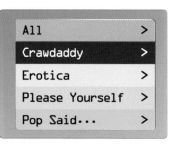

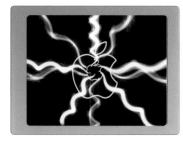

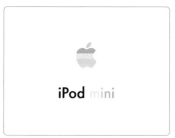

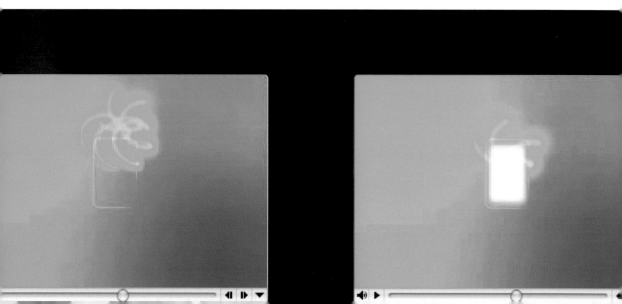

Sausage-Straddling Dominatrix iPod Skins

When the giant computer company Hewlett-Packard started reselling HP-branded iPods in 2004, it tried to distinguish itself from Apple by offering customers a range of stick-on covers called Tattoos. Like cell-phone faceplates, the stickers allow customers to personalize their device. The idea is popular, and several companies sell similar stick-ons.

MacSkinz, for example, commissioned well-known illustrators and comic artists to produce iPod covers. Limited to runs of 100 units, the Artist Series PodSkinz were designed by the likes of poster artist Frank Kozik; illustrator couple Susan and Allen Crawford (Plankton Art); pin-up designer Andrew Bawidamann; illustrator Dave Johnson; and German designer/graffiti artist Neck.CNS. The designs are edgier that anything Apple and HP have attempted: like Dave Johnson's weiner-riding dominatrix, for example.

"My goal with the artist series is to get quite a few artists on board from different styles: low brow, pop art, comics, contemporary, graffiti,

et cetera," said MacSkinz owner Doug Griffith. "This will enable me to promote PodSkinz outside the computer industry, and it should give exposure to the artists in otherwise untapped areas as well." The "skinz" are snap-on plastic covers for late-model iPods. About the thickness of a credit card, the skinz come in halves, held in place by a pair of sticky strips running up each side. Griffith promises more designs. "There are many artists on board that are not yet visible online but should be shortly, as I receive their art," he said.

Hewlett-Packard is exploring similar territory with a series of Tattoo iPod stick-ons by noted fashion designers.

(ABOVE) MacSkinz commissioned dozens of well-known artists and illustrators to design limited edition stick-on iPod "skinz." CREDIT: MACSKINZ; (NEXT PAGE) Illustrator Dave Johnson, aka Devilpig, designed this iPod stick-on "skin" featuring a weiner-riding dominatrix. CREDIT: DAVE JOHNSON/MACSKINZ

"THE **MAC PLATFORM,** AND THE **iPOD**, HAVE CREATED A **CORE FOLLOWING,** A CUSTOMER **PASSION**."

iPOD FANS GET INTO THE PICTURE

Not only are iPod users making their own ads for Apple Computer, they're turning themselves *into* ads for Apple. An independent web-based service iPod My Photo transforms any digital photo into a signature iPod silhouette-style ad. Customers upload a digital snap, choose a background color, and pay. In about five days, they get back the "iPodified" image, which almost always includes a white iPod and earbud wires added where none appeared before. The service has proven wildly successful. A week after launch, the site received orders for about 150 iPodified images. "It's mostly pets, a lot of children, and tons of married couples," said iPod My Photo cofounder Kevin Muoio. "There's lots of new babies, too. Straight out of the womb—bang, they've got an iPod on them."

The iPod My Photo service is the brainchild of Muoio, a 34-year-old salesman from Rhode Island, and his friend Dave Schroeder, 35, a web developer who lives in Virginia. "It's far exceeded our expectations," said Muoio. "We're getting some amazing feedback. There's been an absolutely ecstatic response." The pair got the idea after noticing all the iPod parodies on the Web. One suggested the silhouette style would make for interesting holiday cards, and a business idea was born. A few weeks later, they were offering the service over the Web using contract Photoshop artists—mostly design students in Canada.

"The demand is pretty overwhelming," said Diego Maclean, iPod My Photo's lead designer. "I've got two associates here in Vancouver that are iPodifying as well. We're putting in long hours, but the variety of photos we receive…keeps it fun."

Muoio said orders are coming from all over the world, mainly the United States, the United Kingdom, and Japan. "Why are people doing this?" he asked. "The iPod is a friggin' phenomenon. It's becoming an

 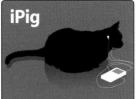

Pets are a popular subject for iPod My Photo's iPod-style silhouette ads. **CREDIT**: COURTESY OF iPODMYPHOTO.COM

icon. It's like Kleenex—every MP3 player will be called an iPod. It's amazing and exciting. It's what's hot right now." Customers are using the images for holiday cards, gift tags, and lots of T-shirts, Muoio said. They've received plenty of wedding photos, sent by friends wanting an unusual holiday gift for the couple in the picture.

"It's a very creative idea from this little company," said Jackie Huba, co-author of *Creating Customer Evangelists* (Dearborn Trade, 2002) and the Church of the Customer website. Huba said the testimonials on the site indicate that some customers want the image to accompany an iPod gift. Others use the image to demonstrate their love of the product or to make a connection with other iPod fans. "The type of people who would use this service are mostly iPod customer evangelists who are attracted to ways to showcase their love for a product that has changed their life," she said. "If people are passionate about a product, they can't get enough of things that are peripheral to that product," she added. "Much like teenagers who love a movie, they buy a poster, the action figures, and soundtrack and join the movie's website bulletin board."

The entrepreneurs are delighted with the public's response, but are a little worried about Apple's reaction. "We hope Apple will be cool and see this as an extension of, er, the power of the iPod, and not someone trying to make a buck on their brand," Muoio said. Muoio said the only complaints he's received are from designers who think $20 is too much for an operation anyone with image-editing software can perform. "If you work in design, it's really friggin' easy," Muoio admitted. "But ask someone who is over 50 to do it, and it's not easy. It's not easy unless you've got the skills."

iPod My Photo will even add white iPods and earbud wires where none were before. **CREDIT**: COURTESY OF iPODMYPHOTO.COM

Customers upload a digital snap choose a background color and pay. Five days later, a custom, handmade iPod ad is e-mailed back. **CREDIT**: COURTESY OF iPODMYPHOTO.COM

Happy Holidays from Tony and Victor.

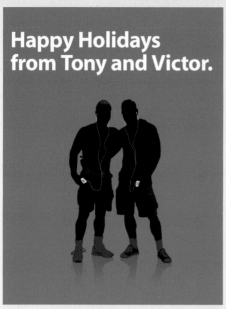

iPod Stewart

rPod.

The service is popular with families looking for an unusual holiday card motif. Mom, dad, and two kids make the perfect (iPod) family.
CREDIT: iPODMYPHOTO.COM

No fear.

Timster - Rockin' & Rollin'

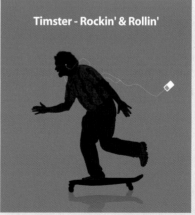

iPod
Snobs Unite

You Were First, Don't Let Them Forget It

In 2004 the Diesel Sweeties web comic started selling a T-shirt that read: "I had an iPod before you even knew what one was."

CELEBRITY iPODS

The iPod has also received a big boost from celebrities. Scads of stars have been pictured in the tabloids with their little white music players, from soccer star David Beckham, Europe's most famous athlete, to Shaquille O'Neal, America's most famous athlete. Apple has also issued several celebrity-endorsed special edition iPods.

In addition to the U2 iPod, which is a special black iPod with the band members' signatures on the back, the iPod has come in limited editions from skateboarder Tony Hawk and pop stars Madonna, Beck, and No Doubt.

(**ABOVE**) One of the world's most famous athletes, soccer star David Beckham, trains with his iPod mini. This kind of endorsement is worth millions. CREDIT: DAVIDBECKHAMPAGES.NET; (**FACING PAGE**) At the 2004 MTV Video Music Awards, hip-hop superstar Sean "P. Diddy" Combs was presented with a diamond-encrusted iPod by Hewlett-Packard. Combs's iPod is covered in more than 120 diamonds; he also received a matching diamond-covered docking cradle. CREDIT: ON THE SCENE PRODUCTIONS

KARL LAGERFELD'S iPOD COLLECTION

Celebrities not only have endorsed the iPod, they also collect them avidly. King of the iPod fanatics is fashion designer Karl Lagerfeld, whose iPod collection numbered 70 at last count. That's right: 70 iPods."I have some white ones but lots of metallic pinks, blues. I had every single CD I have downloaded [onto them]. I enjoy gadgets," Lagerfeld told the U.K.'s *Daily Telegraph* in December 2004, which totaled them up.

Lagerfeld has converted his collection of 60,000 compact discs to a unique iPod storage system, according to a report in *Women's Wear Daily*. Lagerfeld keeps most of the iPods scattered around his various homes, which, in turn, are scattered around the globe. "The iPod completely changed the way people approach music," Lagerfeld told *WWD*. The report continues, "The technology also inspired him to create iPod carrying cases for Fendi, and he allowed that [the iPod's] shape and materials could also be inspiring for fashion in general."

The iPod's influence can indeed be seen throughout Lagerfeld's 2004 collection for Fendi, which includes the ultimate iPod accessory: a $1,500 carrying case for transporting multiple iPods called the Juke Box. The carrying case, unveiled at a catwalk show in Milan, is a rectangular gilded purse about the size of a bread bin. It is lined with multicolored cloth and incorporates a pocket for holding up to a dozen iPods. The Juke Box is modeled after Lagerfeld's own iPod carrying case, an antique leather case "monogrammed for some Jazz Age aristocrat," according to a description by Hamish Bowles, *Vogue*'s European editor-at-large.

Lagerfeld uses the antique leather case to stow his multiple iPods. When he talked to Bowles, Lagerfeld's collection of iPods numbered a mere dozen, which contained about 120,000 tracks, all of which he seemed to know where to find, Bowles reported. Lest this be taken as a joke, it is not. The purse is designed specifically as an iPod carrying case. There's even a hole on one side for the iPod's earpiece cable. "It was designed for the iPod," confirmed Fendi spokeswoman Ayana Lewis, who is based in New York.

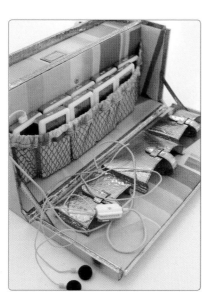

Fendi's Juke Box is a $1,500 carrying case for transporting up to a dozen iPods. Designer Karl Lagerfeld modeled it on his own iPod case, which he uses to transport his collection of 70 iPods

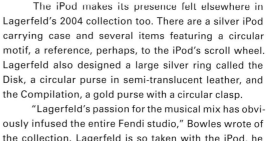

The iPod makes its presence felt elsewhere in Lagerfeld's 2004 collection too. There are a silver iPod carrying case and several items featuring a circular motif, a reference, perhaps, to the iPod's scroll wheel. Lagerfeld also designed a large silver ring called the Disk, a circular purse in semi-translucent leather, and the Compilation, a gold purse with a circular clasp.

"Lagerfeld's passion for the musical mix has obviously infused the entire Fendi studio," Bowles wrote of the collection. Lagerfeld is so taken with the iPod, he often steers interviews toward talk of Apple's technology; at least, that's the running joke on French websites such as MacBidouille. But although Lagerfeld may have use for a giant gilded iPod suitcase, it is unclear why he feels Fendi customers need or want a giant carrying case for multiple music players. Unfortunately, Fendi in Rome did not respond to repeated requests for more information or an interview with Lagerfeld.

Fendi is not the only fashion house to introduce expensive and luxurious iPod accessories. Most of the major international design houses sell iPod cases, including Pucci, Dior, Chanel, and Coach. The famous Colette boutique in Paris sells several styles too. Gucci's iPod Sling is a $200 carrying case with leather trim and silver clasps. Anya Hindmarch's bespoke Ebury handbag, a hot item in society circles, has a special compartment just for the iPod. "The same consumer who buys an iPod buys luxury goods," Floriane de Saint Pierre, a Parisian fashion-industry headhunter, told the *International Herald Tribune*.

"It's a hot gadget right now, and these designers don't want to miss the boat," said Janet Ozzard, executive editor of Style.com, the online home of *Vogue* and *W*. Ozzard said she saw the same thing with cell phones. As the gadgets grew ubiquitous, designers quickly turned out expensive and luxurious carrying cases and accessories. If these high-end consumers needed the electronic device with them all the time, they would use it to make a fashion statement. Danika Cleary, Apple's iPod product manager, said, "The iPod has become iconic, and fashion designers have picked up on it. It's a fashion item in itself."

COOL HUNTERS LIKE APPLE'S SHINE

Thanks to the iPod, Apple is one of the hottest companies in youth culture, according to so-called cool hunters, researchers who track buying trends among young people. "Apple comes up consistently in our research," said DeeDee Gordon, co-president of Look-Look, a youth marketing and research firm in Los Angeles. "Apple is one of the top five brands for young people." According to Gordon, the only other companies mentioned as much by young people are Nike, Target, VW, and Sony. "Apple comes up as a favorite brand, something they're saving up to buy, even a fashion accessory," she said.

Gordon, herself a Mac user, said Apple appeals to young people because celebrities they perceive as cool, including musicians, filmmakers, and designers, use its products. She also said Apple's slick advertising contributes to that image, as do its upscale retail stores. "[Apple] came out with the first cool-looking computer that matched [young people's] sensibilities," she said. "The iMac was [Apple's] entrée into youth culture. It took them to a whole other place in youth culture. The iPod is another cool product from a cool company."

To conduct its research, Look-Look queries a worldwide network of 20,000 Net-connected correspondents ages 13 to 35 years old. Asked recently what company they would most like to endorse (if they were a celebrity), the correspondents nominated Apple the most popular choice, followed by Coca-Cola, Levi's, and Nike. Look-Look also asked its network about "cool new gadgets." Picture-taking cell phones topped the list, followed by the iPod and Sony's PlayStation. But when it came to "extremely well designed products," Apple's iMac and iPod were voted No. 1.

Claire Brooks, executive research director of the Lambesis Research Group, which publishes the *L Style Report*, a quarterly tip sheet, also said Apple is mentioned consistently in its research. "(Apple) is a core trendsetter brand," she said. "It's a lifestyle thing. Apple just comes up all the time." Like Look-Look, Lambesis maintains a network of in-the-field researchers but concentrates on young people deemed trendsetters, or "urban pioneers." Ages 15 to 34, though most are in their mid-20s, these trendsetters make the key brand choices that influence everyone else, Brooks said. Brooks said Apple is one of the top brands among trendsetters, along with Nokia, Sony Ericsson, and Nike. In the last four editions of the *L Style Report*, Apple products have been covered twice, "which is a lot," Brooks said.

Barbara Coulon, vice president of trends at Youth Intelligence, a New York trend-forecasting firm, said the iPod is primarily responsible for Apple's high profile among young people. Youth Intelligence also focuses on trendsetters, maintaining an online panel of about 1,000 trendsetters who are constantly quizzed about what's hot and what's not.

Another index of cool is sales. Although Apple and Dell are the only two PC companies posting a profit these days, Apple hasn't shown signs of explosive growth, despite predictions that the iPod's popularity would bring more customers to the entire Apple product line. Unfortunately for Apple, the company's coolness will always be tied to niche market share, according to Alex Wipperfürth, principal of San Francisco marketing company Plan B and author of *Brand Hijack* (Portfolio, 2005), a book on cult brands. "There will always be a correlation between a product's coolness and niche market share," Wipperfürth said. "By definition, being cool is the opposite of being mainstream, and as long as a brand has a cool cachet, it will remain small."

iPOD USERS IN THE CLOSET

The iPod's telltale white earbuds are a blessing and a curse for Apple. The distinctive earbuds helped propel the iPod to prominence, but may become a millstone if the iPod is deemed passé. Author and speaker Seth Godin is on his fifth iPod, but he's never once worn the white earbuds. Why not? Because Godin doesn't want to be recognized as an iPod owner. Godin is a closet iPod user, one of a small cadre of iPod lovers loath to be identified as an iPod lover.

Closet users such as Godin can't stand the way the earbuds scream, "Woo hoo, look at me, I've got an iPod!"

"I'm not looking forward to being identified on the street," Godin said. "I don't know why. I don't like it."

As the iPod moves fast into the mainstream, more and more users are going into the closet. "I started to feel like a walking iPod ad," said one New Yorker, who preferred to remain anonymous, in print and in person. "I actually dug out an old pair of black headphones to use with mine."

To some closet iPod owners, using nonwhite headphones is a reaction to the growing hordes of iPod fans clogging the sidewalks and subways. Others don't like wearing corporate logos at all, even earbuds.

Godin, who lives in New York, said he knows plenty of other New Yorkers who also refuse to wear the white earpieces. Most rationalize it, he said, by saying they get better audio from different headphones. But in reality, they're asserting their individuality. "It makes me feel individual to customize it," Godin said. "Even if it's just changing the headphones. That's the irony of the whole thing. Most of the people who are Apple's biggest cheering section are people who go out of their way to wear what everyone else is not wearing and eat where not everyone else is eating. They're the kind of people who like to customize their life and feel like they're independent."

The Real iPod Demographic

Like the iPod itself, Apple's TV ads for the device are simple and distinctive. The same aesthetic is at work: a basic color scheme and a great choice of music, not too popular but not too obscure either. The ads use silhouette figures to highlight the white earbuds, but have the added benefit of making the dancers anonymous — they are everyman and everywoman. The ads make it seem like iPod users are hip youngsters. But the real demographic is skewed a lot older; owners are most likely male, aged between 30 and 40, and financially comfortable, according to a 2005 survey by Pew Internet & American Life Project.

Rock it.

CREDIT: iPODMYPHOTO

Across the pond, the iPod demographic is defined by what the UK music industry calls "the 50-Quid Bloke." The 50-Quid Bloke is an aging music fanatic who spends 50 quid (about $100) every week on CDs and DVDs. In an age of digital downloads, the 50-Quid Bloke is seen as the savior of the music industry. Unlike his younger counterparts, he isn't spending all his time downloading copyright music off the Net, and he's more inclined to spend his cash on CDs than ringtones.

For the first time in the UK, more than half the albums sold today are bought by people over 40, according numbers published by *The Guardian* from the British Phonographic Industry. "The generation gap, once about content, has shifted to modes of consumption," says *The Guardian.* "For the under-30s, music is something to be shared and swapped and downloaded, legally or otherwise. It doesn't need to be owned because it's everywhere. If they do buy it, it may be in a form as slight as a mobile ringtone. This terrifies the music business, which can see itself slipping beneath the waves. With Dido and Norah Jones ruling the album chart, the Beatles and Led Zeppelin selling plenty of DVDs, Duran Duran and Tears for Fears suddenly returning from oblivion and Franz Ferdinand achieving instant success, it looks as if the 50-Quid Bloke is keeping the music business afloat."

The average iPod user is more likely to be north of 40 than a hip teenager.
CREDIT: LEANDER KAHNEY

Closet iPod use is particularly acute among early adopters, said consumer behaviorist Tom O'Guinn, because they don't want to be identified with the Johnny-come-latelies. "The phenomenon in question is 'desired marginality,'" he said. O'Guinn explained that, for some Mac users, for example, Apple's marginal status and low market share is a "source of pride." And as the iPod goes mainstream, some early adopters are affronted by its lack of exclusivity.

Michael Bull, a lecturer in media and culture at the University of Sussex in the United Kingdom (for more information on Bull, see Chapter 2), concurred.

"As iPods become more popular, so their cultural cachet is reduced," Bull said. "Quite a few U.S. users note with alarm the increase in numbers of iPods they see in the streets. Before, there was a kind of specialness in recognizing another early adopter, a recognition of cultural superiority."

Drew Neisser, president and CEO of Renegade Marketing Group, a New York advertising firm, said Apple has been working hard to keep the iPod fresh and fashionable and may eventually offer different-colored earbuds to distinguish different groups of users. "Apple is at a critical fork in the road when it comes to the iPod," he wrote in an email. "You can already begin to see the initial iPod pioneers, who embraced the value of individuality, shunning the storm of homogeneity that's growing with each new purchase."

But if some hipsters and early adopters are clandestine about their iPod ardor, is the iPod in any danger of becoming unfashionable? Several professional style watchers say not likely: The iPod couldn't be more fashionable. Editor Brooks of *L Style Report* said, "It's no longer particularly hip to own an iPod, but it's definitely not passé either. The iPod has moved from hip accessory to lifestyle classic almost immediately, which is something very few brands are able to do, and certainly none of the competitive offerings ... The only people I've met who are closet users are middle-aged ex-college rockers who have a guilt complex about rediscovering the bad-boy tunes of their youth," she said.

Janet Ozzard of Style.com said the iPod isn't even close to becoming un-hip. "Most people I know are so in love with theirs that they spend weekends hanging out at the Apple store in SoHo stocking up on accessories," she said.

DeeDee Gordon of Look-Look said hipsters are fully aware that the iPod is no longer cutting-edge, but it's not a deterrent.

Blogger Josh Rubin, who publishes Cool Hunting, said it's "totally hip" to own an iPod. "I don't know of anyone who is embarrassed," he said. "There's a whole white-cord subculture here in NYC. It's like an unspoken brother/sisterhood on the subways and in the streets." Rubin, however, admitted he personally doesn't use the white headphones—for reasons of better audio quality, naturally. "So I guess I'm proud," he said, "but stealth."

Author Godin related a revealing story about a friend who became "very upset" with the white earbuds. "He felt he was being used by Apple," Godin said. "Everyone who got on the subway, he got that look. So he got a pair of black earbuds." Godin continued, "He gets on the subway, being very independent and a maverick, which is what New Yorkers like to do, and he sees another guy across the car wearing black headphones. And this guy pulls out an iPod to adjust the volume. My friend catches himself giving this guy *the look*, the I've-got-an-iPod-too wink." Godin concluded, "It proves people like it when they find other people like them. People who don't like being part of the main tribe still like being part of a smaller tribe."

II   Now Playing   [████]

5 of 8

iPod, uPod,
Everybody iPod

0:00   -5:46

MENU

TURN UP

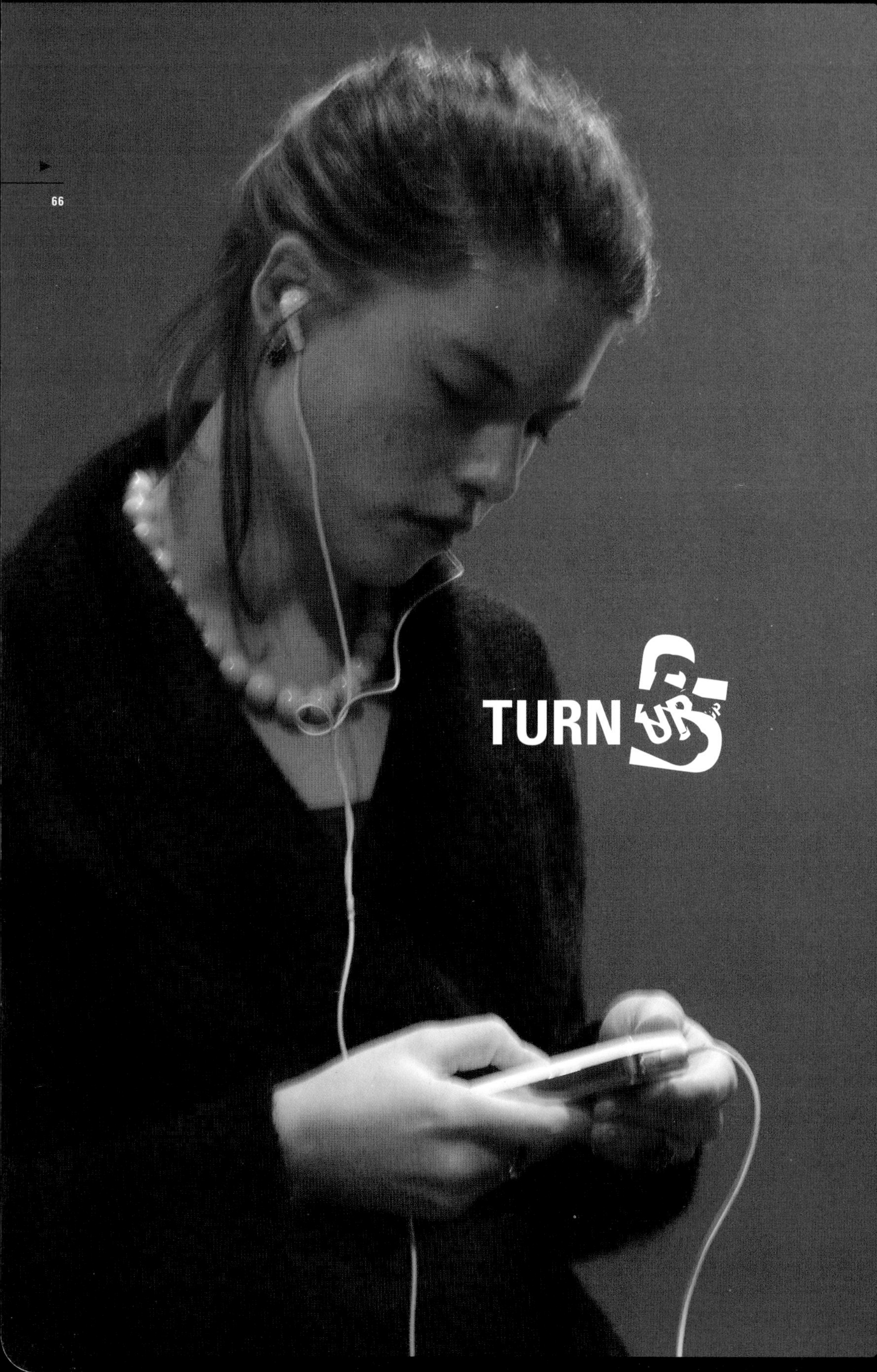

TUNE IN

DANCE OUT

(THIS PAGE & PREVIOUS SPREAD)
B.Y.O. iPod: Dancers are the DJs at Holland's iDJ iPodparty in the GEM museum in The Hague in November 2004. **CREDIT:** EBBERT OLIEROOK

MP3Js

In cities all over the world, dancers are becoming DJs, thanks to the iPod. Instead of hiring a DJ, clubs and pubs are setting up simple mixing desks with a pair of iPods loaded with thousands of tracks. Patrons then take turns selecting songs for everyone else to dance to. You-are-the-DJ iPod party nights started in New York shortly after the iPod was first released and have since spread to most major cities—and to a lot of smaller ones.

London's weekly Playlist party, for example, is held every Saturday at the trendy Nambucca club on Holloway Road. "Playlist celebrates digital diversity," the club proclaims on its website. "The principle is simple: if you want to share your music, just turn up, sign in, and play out. If you want to judge other people's music, turn up, sign up, and speak out. If you simply want to party, just turn up, tune in, dance it out.

WITH AN iPOD, WHO NEEDS A TURNTABLE?

One of the first clubs to swap DJs for iPods was New York's APT. (pronounced A-P-T), a trendy lounge in Manhattan's Meat Packing District. The club resembles an upscale Manhattan apartment—but much bigger. Next to the bar is the DJ table. The set-up revolves around a standard mixer connected to a pair of iPods.

Everyone gets to play. Would-be DJs take a numbered ticket from a deli-style dispenser. Printouts of all the songs are available to help DJs prepare a set list. "Playing of any heavy metal ballads will result in immediate expulsion from the premises," the printout warns. With thousands of songs to choose from, patrons play everything from Black Sabbath to Basement Jaxx. Sets last seven minutes; the remaining time is counted down on a big digital clock.

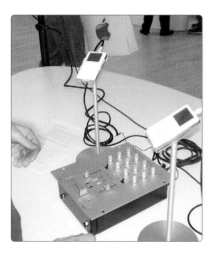

(LEFT) Connect a pair of iPods to a standard mixing console, and you have an easy-to-use mix desk with thousands of songs at the DJ's fingertips. CREDIT: iLOUNGE; (ABOVE) Team Pod: New York's trendy APT. bar allows patrons to be the DJ. The nightclub has set up a pair of iPods. Patrons take a ticket, deli style, and when their number comes up, they get seven minutes of dance floor fame. CREDIT: APT

The iPod setup provides hours of boozy, gregarious fun. Half the bar crowds around the mixing desk, offering advice or criticism or just dancing away. "It gets pretty crazy," said Sai Blount, the lounge's music promoter. "We have people yelling. Some people boo. A couple of girls came in here three or four weeks in a row. They got really good. They were like professional."

Matt Maland, a 27-year-old part-time DJ, is a semiregular. He's even figured out how to make the iPods scratch. By pressing the center button twice in quick succession, the music backs up a fraction. "It's fun," he said. "It's different. It's a challenge. You have to think what songs go together more than vinyl because you can't beat-match."

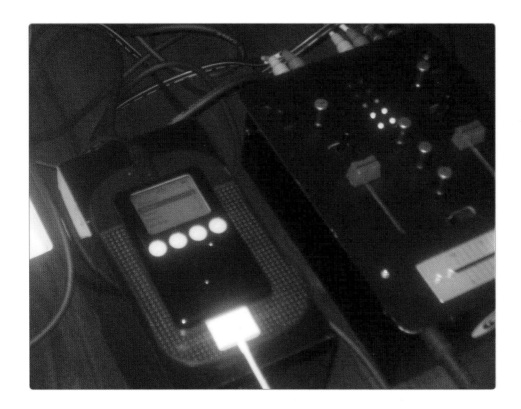

ANDREW ANDREW (THEY WALK ALIKE, THEY DJ ALIKE)

Andrew Andrew, a pair of New York DJs, were among the first club DJs to swap bulky boxes of records for Apple's compact iPods. The pair tote a pair of iPods to gigs at galleries, parties, and clubs all over town. They host a regular Tuesday night event, the iParty, at APT.

Even by New York standards, Andrew Andrew are eccentric. They dress identically, have the same haircut, and wear the same glasses. The pair met at Disneyland about three years ago. Andrew approached Andrew and asked him, "Mac or IBM?" "It's the pivotal question of our time," Andrew said.

They look like twins but are, in fact, merely business partners. Their company, Andrew Andrew, is a registered partnership with a diverse line of products. They DJ, play in a band, curate art shows, have a clothing line, and design home furnishings. Wherever they go, heads turn. They attract intense curiosity. Once, someone actually got mad, accusing them of *impersonating* twins.

For attention seekers, they are quite reserved, almost shy. They refuse to divulge any distinguishing information—last names, birthdays, backgrounds. They always wear the same outfits. Their haircuts are cropped short. They drink the same vodka tonics, and when they smoke, Andrew lights two cigarettes. Like twins, they finish each other's sentences. They carry identical iPods, cell phones, Palm handhelds, and wallets. "When you're with someone a lot, you start to talk alike," explained one of the Andrews.

Andrew Andrew live together in an apartment on Staten Island that doubles as their office. Their wardrobe contains two of everything, arranged by color. They've discarded everything that doesn't match. Their toiletries are paired. Their library contains two of each book, which they read simultaneously. They have the same tattoo of Mario, the Nintendo game character, on their right arms. They eat the same food. "In seven years we'll be chemically exact," the other Andrew said.

The pair work as DJs at art galleries and nightclubs. They used to dress as mad scientists in white lab coats to match the iPods, but switched to black iPods and black lab coats when the black U2 iPod came out.

They play an eclectic set. They choose a word—say *sex*, *work*, or *world*—and play songs containing the word in the artist's name, song title, or lyrics. It makes for a diverse mix: opera, pop, rockabilly, techno, and dozens of other styles. It doesn't always go over too well with the dance crowd. In fact, this brand of DJing works best at art galleries, where the crowds are more tolerant of eccentricity. At one nightclub gig, in fact, Andrew Andrew were asked to leave after just 30 minutes. But, as they've become better known, people have started to catch on.

Naturally, the Andrews' iPods contain the same songs. Before the iPods, they DJed with 15 to 20 preburned CDs and a hand-written set list. The iPods have vastly simplified the process. "We've been DJing differently from other DJs from the get-go," said Andrew. "So for us, the iPod is perfect. A lot of people don't like the songs, but for the DJ, it's perfect."

Over time, Apple has transformed the iPod from a simple audio player into a general-purpose digital assistant, capable of storing contacts and calendars, games, email, and even entire novels—as well as giga-bytes of music. It's possible that Apple had planned from the start to make the iPod into an ersatz PDA, but it's also possible the company took its lead from iPod hackers, who, almost from the minute the gadget hit store shelves, were busy figuring out clever ways of making the iPod do more than just play music. In the first few weeks after the iPod's debut, hackers figured out how to store not only names and addresses on the iPod but calendar items, news stories, song lyrics, and phrases in foreign languages. One enterprising teen even worked out a way to steal software using his iPod. (See the section "Have iPod, Will Secretly Bootleg," later in this chapter.)

Some inventive iPod owners even got their play-ers to work with Windows before the release of Apple's sanctioned Windows-compatible version. Joe Masters, a student at Williams College in Massachusetts, wrote a free program called EphPod to connect iPods to Win-dows machines.

It took Apple six months to catch up with the hackers. Half a year after its initial release, Apple updated the iPod's software to let it store contacts. The iPod software has the ability to download thousands of contacts from applications such as Microsoft's Entourage (the Macintosh version of Outlook), Palm's desktop, and the Mac OS X address book. But hackers also figured out how to make it work with other contact databases, including Yahoo's online address book.

Jean-Olivier Lanctôt-David, a 14-year-old hacker from Canada, figured out a way to display online news headlines on the iPod. Lanctôt-David whipped up Pod-News, a program that fetches headlines from the Web in XML format and displays them on the iPod's small screen. It's quite an achievement, especially for a young teen.

After Apple added contacts, iPod hackers turned to calendar functions. A French hacker created K-Landar, which displays calendar events, such as a list of meet-ings, as an iPod playlist. Events can be set by time, category, comments, or description.

Michael Zapp, an instructor at the University of Manitoba in Canada, created a pair of AppleScript applications to take data from Microsoft's Entourage and transform it into vCard file format, which can be displayed using the iPod's new contacts feature. One of Zapp's scripts extracts events, allowing the iPod to display schedules; the other extracts text notes, which can display any kind of information. "I've had people say that they may just retire their Palm since they can now do everything they use it for with the iPod and my apps," said Zapp. "I think people are tired of carrying around lots of gadgets and are looking for anything that can reduce the load." The only problem, Zapp said, is that information can't be entered when the iPod is away from a Mac; all data has to be typed into a Mac and transferred manually.

EphPod creator Joe Masters said the iPod had great potential as an organizer, particularly because it's much easier to program than Palm devices. "It's got so much space, and it's very easy to hack," he said. "Apple's done a great job. It's very simple. Synchronizing it is very easy. It's just a hard drive. You just copy files over. There are no weird synchronization protocols like the Palm. And you don't have to worry about space, like on a Palm. It's enormous. Who cares how much space you use?"

iPod hackers also figured out all kinds of undocumented tips and tricks, including a diagnostic mode that checks the iPod's internal hard drive, among other things. VersionTracker, a popular software-download website, lists more than several dozen hacks for the iPod. The hacks provide clues to the future direction of the iPod. "No doubt Apple is taking its cue from some of these hacks," said Blake Patterson, who runs the iPodHacks website. "Apple is seeing that a lot of users want these kinds of organizer functions." Apple didn't respond to requests for comment.

…ALMOST FROM THE MINUTE [THE iPOD] HIT STORE SHELVES, [HACKERS] WERE BUSY FIGURING OUT CLEVER WAYS OF MAKING THE iPOD DO MORE…

(THIS PAGE) Pod Person: Jean-Olivier Lanctôt-David, a 14-year-old hacker from Canada, and a screenshot of his PodNews program, which fetches headlines from the Web in XML format and displays them on the iPod's small screen. CREDIT: LANCTÔT-DAVID

(FACING PAGE) iPod Nut: Joe Masters (on the left in photo) and his college buddies enjoy some doughnuts. Masters wrote EphPod, which connects iPods to Windows machines (screenshot to right). CREDIT: JOE MASTERS

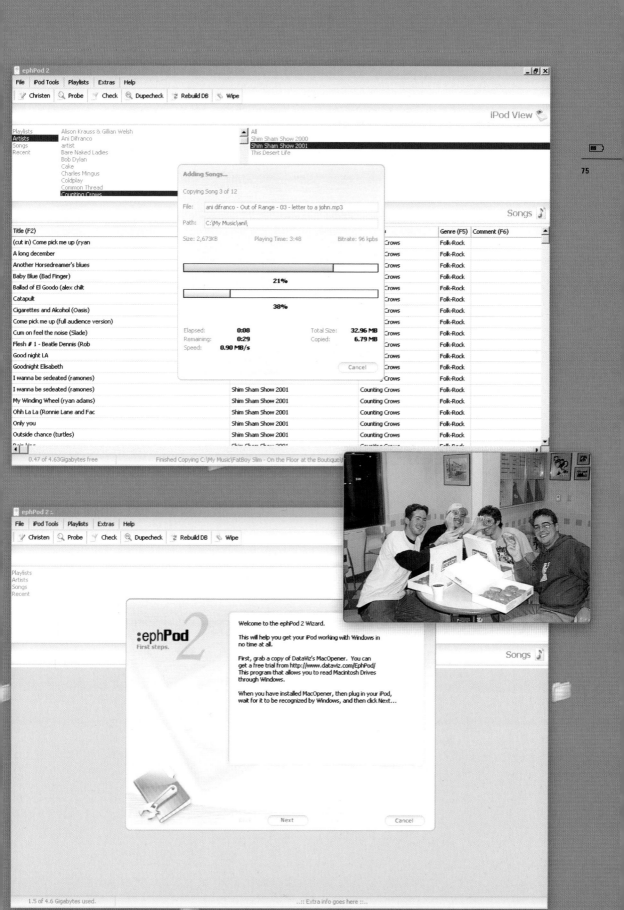

CREDIT: JIM WRIGHT

Shuffle Drive: Connect four iPod shuffles to a USB hub, and what do you have? A very slow USB storage drive.

World's Slowest RAID

Jim Wright has four friends, each of whom own an iPod shuffle. Wright persuaded them to pool their resources to make a 4GB RAID (Redundant Arrays of Inexpensive Disks) storage device. Wright connected the shuffles to a four-port USB 2 hub and format-ted it with disk utility software. The setup worked, but it's no speed demon. It took nearly 11 minutes to copy just under 2GB of data.

Double Vision: Astrophysicist Paul Bourke updated an antique stereoscope with a pair of iPod photos. **CREDIT**: PAUL BOURKE

World's First (and Only) iPod Stereoscope

Australian astrophysicist Paul Bourke has constructed what must be the only stereo-scope made from a pair of iPod photos. The stereoscope is an Edwardian inven-tion that conjures a 3D image from two photographs of the same scene taken from slightly different angles. When each image is presented to a different eye, the brain fuses them into a 3D scene: it's the principle of ste-reo vision. Bourke's iPod photo stereoscope uses iPods instead of photo-graphs to present images to each eye. Naturally, he has to take two slightly skewed images of a scene with a digital camera and be sure to load the correct image onto the correct iPod.

Homemade
Shuffle
Shades

Oakley, a popular sunglasses brand, sells eyewear that doubles as a music player: the MP3 Thump. Tinkerer extraordinaire Phillip Torrone, an editor with *Make* magazine, created his own variation using an iPod shuffle. They look better and are cheaper too.

CREDIT: PHILLIP TORRONE

HAVE iPOD, WILL SECRETLY BOOTLEG

When Apple introduced the iPod, the company was aware that people might use it to rip off music. Each new iPod, in fact, is emblazoned with a sticker that warns, "Don't Steal Music." But it is unlikely that Apple imagined people would walk into computer stores, plug their iPod into display computers, and use it to copy software off the hard drives.

This is exactly the scenario recently witnessed by computer consultant Kevin Webb at a Dallas CompUSA store. Webb was browsing when he saw a young man walk toward him listening to an iPod. Webb recognized the iPod's distinctive ear buds.

The teenager stopped at a display Macintosh nearby, pulled the iPod from his pocket, and plugged it into the machine with a FireWire cable. Intrigued, Webb peeped over the kid's shoulder to see him copying Microsoft's new Office for OS X suite, which retailed for $500.

When the iPod is plugged into a Macintosh, its icon automatically pops up on the desktop (if it's set up as an external hard drive, which is easily done). To copy software, all the kid had to do was drag and drop files onto the iPod's icon. Office for Mac OS X is about 200 MB; it copies to the iPod's hard drive in less than a minute. "Watching him, it dawned on me that this was something that was very easy to do," Webb said. "In the Mac world it's pretty easy to plug in and copy things. It's a lot easier than stealing the box." Webb watched the teenager copy a couple of other applications before going off to find a CompUSA employee. "I went over and told a CompUSA guy, but he looked at me like I was clueless," Webb said. Unsure whether the kid was a thief or an out-of-uniform employee, Webb watched as he left the store. "I thought there's no point in getting any more involved in this imbroglio," Webb said. "Besides, this is Texas. You never know what he might have been carrying."

(THIS PAGE LEFT) Saints and Sinners: If only the pious had iPods. Apple foresaw how the iPod could be used to steal music, but the company may not have expected users to steal software from demo machines at computer stores. CREDIT: ONEBISHOP@MAC.COM; (THIS PAGE RIGHT) Mona iPod. The Mona Lisa whiles away the hours in the Louvre, listening to some killer tunes. CREDIT: UNKNOWN; (FACING PAGE) Drag and Dash: Copying software onto an iPod is as easy as drag and drop. CREDIT: LEANDER KAHNEY

The iPod's fast interface—an important but undersold feature—allows huge files to be copied in seconds. The iPod doesn't even have to leave the user's pocket. And although the iPod has a built-in antipiracy mechanism that prevents music files from being copied from one computer to another, it has no such protections for software. Ironically, Microsoft pioneered an easy-to-use installation scheme on the Mac that makes its Mac software relatively simple to pilfer. When installing Office, users simply drag and drop the Office folder to their hard drive. Everything is built in, including a self-repair mechanism that replaces critical files in the system folder.

By contrast, a lot of software for the Windows platform relies on a bunch of system files that are only loaded during an installation process. Simply copying an application from one machine to another will not work on Windows. "This is the first we have heard of this form of piracy," said Erik Ryan, a Microsoft product manager. "And while this is a possibility, people should be reminded that this is considered theft."

Although the iPod may be ideal for a software-stealing spree, a number of other devices on the market could also be used by virtual shoplifters, including any number of external hard drives, such as tiny USB key-chain drives. However, except for those with new USB 2 ports, most key-chain drives are a lot slower than FireWire, requiring the virtual shoplifter to hang around while the ill-gotten loot is transferring. Dennis Lloyd, publisher of iPod fan site iLounge, said he was shocked to hear of an iPod put to such use. "It's a shame someone has stooped this low to bring bad press to the insanely great iPod," he said.

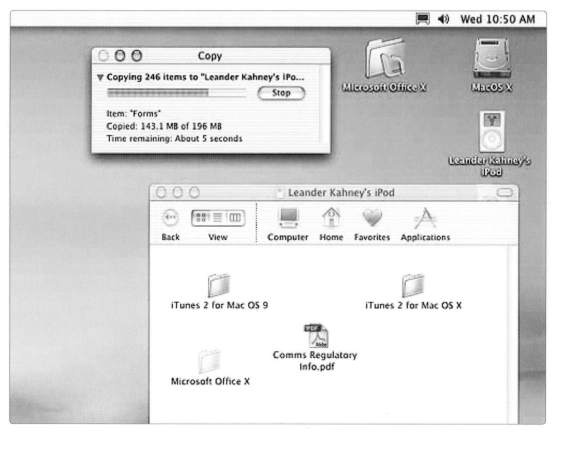

Serial No.: JQ453TQSKK

Designed by Apple in California. Assemb

Model No.: A1051 EMC No.: 1984 Rated 5

TM and © 2004 Apple Computer, Inc.

FC CE VCI

A lot of people are dressing up as iPods at Halloween.
Most of the costumes are fairly basic, but New Yorker
Philip Yee's costume was more elaborate than most.
So realistic was his costume, other revelers in New
York's legendary Halloween parade thought he was an
Apple-sponsored walking advertisement.
Perfect in every detail, his costume even
had a serial number and "Assembled
by P.Yee" on the back. Visiting Apple's
store in SoHo, he attracted a big crowd and was soon
was asked to leave for causing a "disturbance."
"It really takes an Apple fanatic to get all the
details correct," said Yee.

i See

iPod

iPod Man Philip Yee at New York's Halloween parade, where he partied with some silhouette people. **CREDIT:** PHILIP YEE

People

Proposal by iPod

Forget diamonds. Popping the question by iPod is the way to go when proposing marriage these days. Take a Norwegian guy called Yoak, who bought his girlfriend an iPod and had this special message laser-etched on the back:

> Ana my love
> Will you marry me?

After he presented her with the iPod, she said yes, of course.

Yoak reported an Internet forum: "She looked very confused for a few seconds, before she said yes. It all took place during the most fantastic sunset over a snow-covered Oslo." Unfortunately, he couldn't be reached for further comment.

iPod Proposal: A Norwegian called Yoak inscribed a marriage proposal on the back of an iPod. **CREDIT**: LEANDER KAHNEY

iPology

Following the reelection of U.S. president George Bush in 2004, lots of disappointed American voters apologized to the world with a website called Sorry Everybody. The site featured digital pictures of voters—mostly Democrats, presumably—holding up hand-drawn signs expressing regret for the results of the closely contested election. Most read, "Sorry, I tried," or "49 percent of us didn't vote for him." One entry to the website was this clever iPod-inspired apology, or iPology. Note the track number, 1 of 55,949,487, which is the number of U.S. voters, and check out the number of minutes the song has played and those remaining, which translates to four down, four to go.

CREDIT: LEANDER KAHNEY

iPod FM 95.9

An FM transmitter is a popular iPod accessory that allows an iPod to play songs through a car radio. Most are powerful enough to play not just in the owner's car, but also in the vehicles around it. Several people have been broadcasting their own microradio stations from their cars — some even without knowing it. One of these, Brian Johnson, told the BoingBoing website: "I've been running around for the past several months with this bumper sticker on my car, ... I figure that anyone that can read the bumper sticker — on the I-5, at a stoplight — if intrigued could tune in and listen to whatever I'm listening to. No, I don't take requests."

CREDIT: BRIAN JOHNSON

iPods

Customized

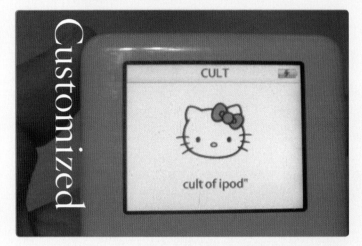

!"#$%'()*+,-./012345
VWXYZ[\]^_'abcdefg
°±²³'¶·,'○≫¼½¾¿Æ
Ŧŧˇ˘°°˙˝~"ΑΒΓΔΕ.
εӡθιϰλϰυξοπρϛτυφχ
ЦЧШЩЪЫЬЭЮЯаб
эюяё-—‖'"""✝✠·…‰
⅓⅔⅛⅜⅝⅞ⅠⅡⅢⅣⅤⅤ
←→↺↥↯↭⇐⇒⇔↕
∠∕∥∧∨∩∪∫∬$·∴∵∷∶
≥≨≷<>⋅⋉⊏⊐⊄⊅⊆
⓪①②③④⑤⑥⑦⑧⑨
⑩⑳ⓐⓑⓒⓓⓔⓕⓖⓗ
⓪ⓣⓤⓥⓗⓙⓚⓜⓝⓞⓞ
╚╝╜╛╙╘├┝┞┟┠┡┢├
┼├┼┼┼┼┼┼┼┼┼
▷▶▼▽◀◁◄◆◇◈
♡♣♤♥♧♨✍♪♫♭♮♯✠✳

!"#$%&'()*+,-./0123456
YZ[\]^_`abcdefghijklmno
ΖΗΘΙΚΛΜΝΞΟΠΡΣΤ
—'""·…ˉ'×⸗˘℃‰℉ᵀᵐ
⁘⁖⁙~≠≒≦≧⊥⊿—⌐¬
■▬▮▪▎▍▊▌▍▐▀□▲◢

!"#$%&'()*+,-./01234!
ЖΥΖ[\]^_`abcdefghijk
²³'μ¶·,¹○≫¼½¾¿ÀÁÂ
æçèéêëìíîïðñòóôõ÷ʍ
êĝğ$ĝǵĝƓÂĥħĦĩ Ĩĩ
ŐŒœŔŕŖŗŘřŚśŜŝŞşŠš
БЬЪɔĆć Ɗɑ∂ℓℨℰ ꬵƒƓ
ΞΠΣΦΧΨΩΪŸἀέήίΰαβʓ
Ḱ℥ṵℾⱮℒℨℽℕℼℸℳℵℱℶℷ
ыьэюяђґєїјљњћ ќ℥ɥ
⁝◇♣ﬀ ﬁ ﬂ ﬃ ﬄ ﬅ ﬆ

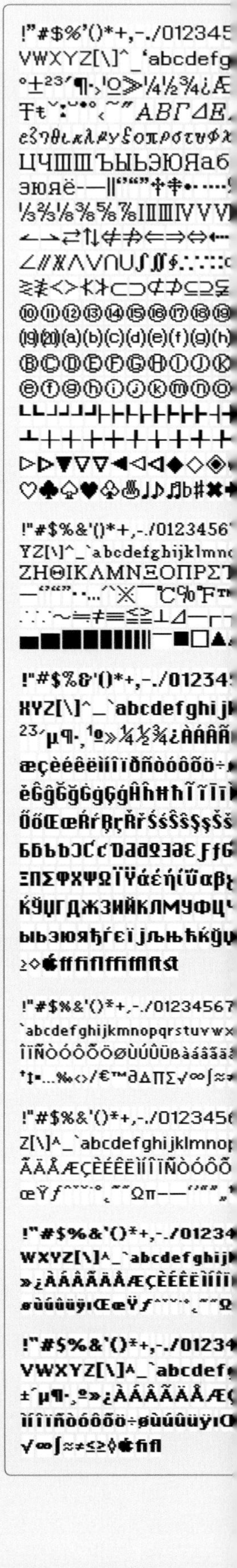

(ABOVE) This customized iPod displays the Hello Kitty logo while the battery charges. **CREDIT**: PHILLIP TORRONE; **(RIGHT)** The various fonts used by the iPod. **CREDIT**: APPLE

An iPod hacker called The Wizard wrote a piece of software that allows custom images to be added to the iPod, like the Hello Kitty logo above. The Wizard's editor can customize the images and fonts in the firmware contained in Apple's iPod software updates. The editor allows users to customize the graphics and then load them onto the iPod when updating the device's software. The editor can also be used to extract all the fonts and images used on the iPod.

!"#$%&'()*+,-./0123456789:;<=>?@ABCDEFGHIJKLMNOPQRSTUVWX
YZ[\]^_`abcdefghijklmnopqrstuvwxyz{|}~

!"#$%&'()*+,-./0123456789:;<=>?@ABCDEFGHIJKLMNOPQRSTUVWX
YZ[\]^_`abcdefghijklmnopqrstuvwxyz{|}~

!"#$%&'()*+,-./0123456789:;<=>?@ABCDEFGHIJKLMNOPQRSTUVWXYZ[\]^_
`abcdefghijklmnopqrstuvwxyz{|}~

!"#$%&'()*+,-./0123456789:;<=>?@ABCDEFGHIJKLMNOPQRSTUVWXYZ[\]^
_`abcdefghijklmnopqrstuvwxyz{|}~

!"#$%&'()*+,-./0123456789:;<=>?@ABCDEFGHIJKLMNOPQRSTUVWX
YZ[\]^_`abcdefghijklmnopqrstuvwxyz{|}~

!"#$%&'()*+,-./0123456789:;<=>?@ABCDEFGHIJKLMNOPQRSTUVW
XYZ[\]^_`abcdefghijklmnopqrstuvwxyz{|}~

!"#$%&'()*+,-./0123456789:;<=>?@ABCDEFGHIJKLMNOPQRSTUVWXYZ[
\]^_`abcdefghijklmnopqrstuvwxyz{|}~

!"#$%&'()*+,-./0123456789:;<=>?@ABCDEFGHIJKLMNOPQRSTUVWX
YZ[\]^_`abcdefghijklmnopqrstuvwxyz{|}~

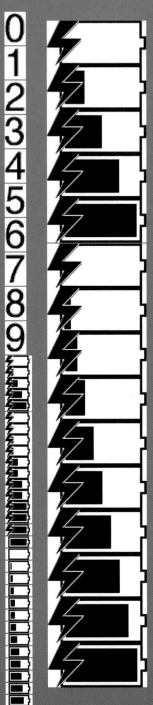

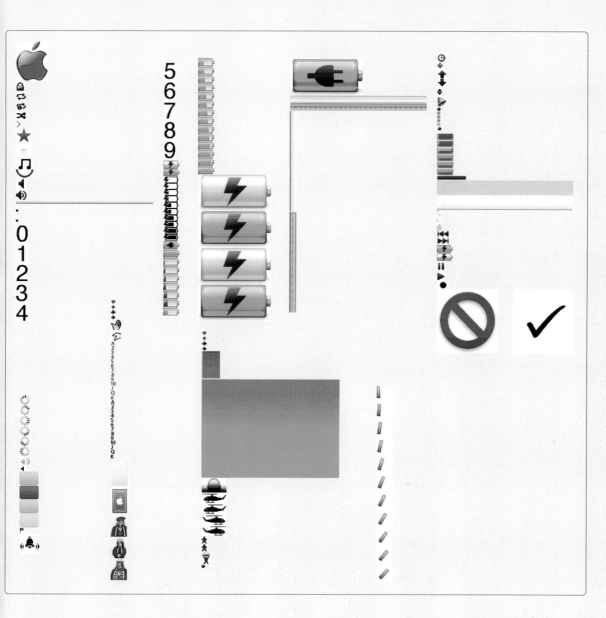

(FACING PAGE) The iPod's graphics. CREDIT: APPLE;

(BELOW) Graphics from the iPod photo, which has a color screen. CREDIT: APPLE

iPod Cozies and Socks

Craft hobbies such as knitting and quilting are sweeping the United States, so it's no surprise that needle workers are crocheting cozies for iPods. The one in the previous illustration was made by someone called Kdka, a 26-year-old woman from Pittsburgh. Her design includes openings for the scroll wheel and LCD screen and even a little pouch in back for storing earbuds.

Another needle worker, LAWebChick, lined her cozy with felt, but the idea needs work. "I found out that felt in combination with an iPod is slippery, and the 'Pod slides right out even if I just have it on the car seat and hit the brakes," she reports.

So popular are iPod cozies that Apple introduced its own. Calling them iPod "Socks," Apple sells a six-pack for $30.

CREDIT: KDKA

iPod Identity Thieves Face the Music

A gang of British identity thieves used an iPod to store digital copies of the documents they needed to buy luxury cars fraudulently, the BBC reported in 2004. False documents and phony identities were used to buy cars under assumed names that were later sold for "pure profit," the BBC said. Apparently, the thieves thought the police wouldn't find the documents if they were stored on an iPod. But the scam came undone when a police officer noticed expensive cars parked at a low-income housing project in London. When police raided a flat there several weeks later, they found the incriminating evidence on the iPod. The gang was sentenced to jail. A police spokesman said they "ended up facing the music."

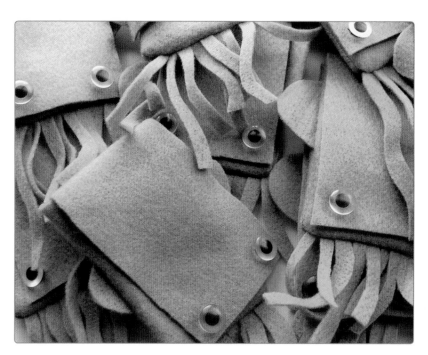

Cephal-iPods

For squid lovers, San Francisco design house Mule Design made a unique cephalopod-shaped iPod case, the Cephal-iPod. Made of felt and costing $20, Mule Design's site says: "Your iPod's glaring whiteness is relaying signals back to the humans. Protect yourself from harmful rays in style with this hand-crafted hip cozy made of (possibly) organic felt."

Says Alaina, "I took the photo after I finished sewing on all their eyes. I love the little guys and wanted to capture a photo of them all together before they were released into the wild and sent to their owners." **CREDIT:** ALAINA BROWNE

The market for iPod accessories has quickly bloomed into a multi-million dollar industry, supplying everything from FM transmitters to iPod socks. **CREDIT**: PHILLIP TORRONE

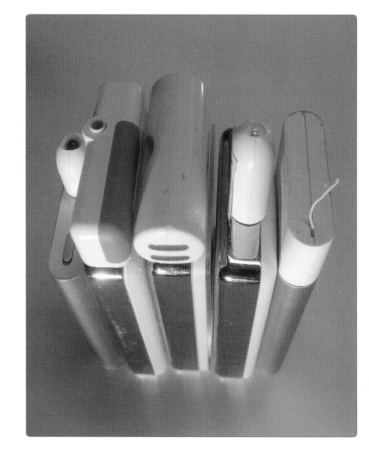

6

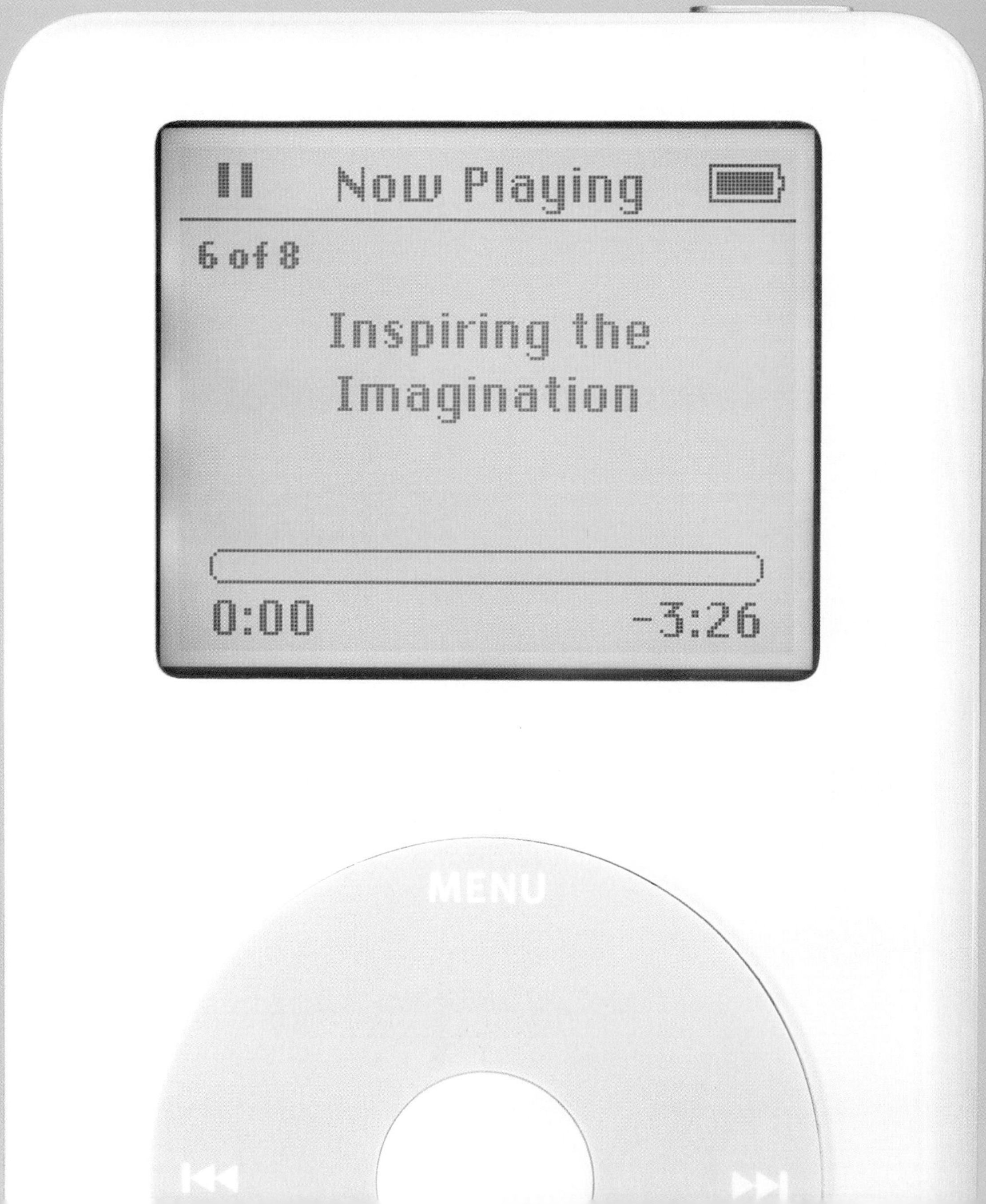

The iPod is the object of a unique tribute: thousands of photos from all over the world showing iPods in exotic locales. The iPods Around the World gallery, part of the iLounge website, has collected more than 3,300 pictures of iPods from all over the globe, from far-flung travel destinations to their owners' backyards. The gallery features pictures of iPods in front of bombed-out palaces in Afghanistan, on jungle expeditions in Peru, and in Mick Jagger's garden in London.

Photos of iPods have been captured on top of mountains, 825 feet below the earth's surface, and inside a Parisian fridge. There are snaps of people with iPods riding a roller coaster in Orlando, Florida, sunbathing in Greece, and giving birth in New York. There are dogs, dogs on motorbikes, lovers, statues, and a nearly naked cowboy—all posing with iPods.

Pictures have been sent from nearly 60 countries, including Vietnam, Turkey, Russia, and Iceland. The gallery was the brainchild of Dennis Lloyd, publisher of iLounge. "I'm surprised that it's been so successful," he said. "But I had a feeling the iPod would take the MP3 world by storm." The gallery is reminiscent of the kidnapped gnome phenomenon—featured in the movie *Amelie*—wherein globetrotters borrow a neighbor's garden decoration and send back picture postcards documenting its travels. "I think some of the best pictures have been those that were from very remote areas or areas that had recently in been in the news," Lloyd said.

THE GALLERY

THE TRAVELING IS LIKE

(ABOVE) Ancient Greece's Parthenon reflected in the back of an iPod. **CREDIT:** YANNI RAFTAKIS;
(LEFT) An iPod on expedition floating the Río Pauya in the Cordillera Azul region of eastern Perú. **CREDIT:** iLOUNGE

1

2

3

4

8

9

10

GNOME

5

6

7

11

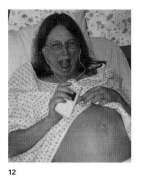

12

13

PHENOMENON

(1) Armany the doggie enjoys listening to his iPod in Noisy Le Roi, France; **(2)** Abraham Lincoln looks down at the iPod from his seat in Chicago, Illinois; **(3)** A fridge in Paris, France; **(4)** The Kuwait Water Towers in Kuwait; **(5)** The Naked Cowboy poses for a pair of iPods in New York's Times Square; **(6)** Sunbathing in Santorini, Greece; **(7)** Zero-to-60 in 2.6 seconds with an iPod on the Disney MGM Rock 'n' Roller Coaster in Orlando, Florida; **(8)** An enhanced iPod photo from the Oakland/Piedmont Rose Gardens in Oakland, California;

(9) Enjoying some Yo-Yo Ma in Kabul, Afghanistan, outside a former palace shelled by various factions for the last 20 years; **(10)** A romantic iPod moment at the Planufer-Cafe in Berlin, Germany; **(11)** 825 feet below the surface at Carlsbad Caverns National Park in Carlsbad, New Mexico; **(12)** An iPod-aided delivery in New York. The expecting mother uses music to calm her angst during the labor pains; **(13)** An iPod in Mick Jagger's garden, London, England **CREDIT:** iLOUNGE

Aural Heaven: iPod and Analog

(1) And Up, a store in the back streets of Tokyo, specializes in selling antique radios and, of all things, iPods. **(2)** And Up is located on the second floor of an old apartment building in an upscale Tokyo neighborhood. **(3)** Takeyuki Ishii, owner of the store, recommends plugging an iPod into an FM transmitter, such as Griffin Technology's iTrip, and listening to music through the speaker of an antique radio. **(4–8)** Store owner Ishii finds aural magic by combining the very old with the very new. Playing an iPod through an antique radio or tube-driven amplifier gives it a special warmth and atmosphere, he says. **CREDIT (ALL PHOTOS):** COURTESY OF NOBUYUKI HAYASHI

1

2

5

6

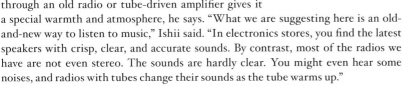

In the back streets of Tokyo's upscale Aoyama district, which is famous for its antique stores, there's a little shop quite unlike the others in the neighborhood. Located on the second floor of an old apartment building, And Up specializes in antique radios and, of all things, iPods. The store's owner, 50-year-old Takeyuki Ishii, recommends plugging an iPod into an FM transmitter and listening to music through the speaker of an antique radio.

Ishii believes there is aural magic in the combination of the very old and the very new. Playing an iPod through an old radio or tube-driven amplifier gives it a special warmth and atmosphere, he says. "What we are suggesting here is an old-and-new way to listen to music," Ishii said. "In electronics stores, you find the latest speakers with crisp, clear, and accurate sounds. By contrast, most of the radios we have are not even stereo. The sounds are hardly clear. You might even hear some noises, and radios with tubes change their sounds as the tube warms up."

Ishii insists the antique equipment creates an atmosphere that has been forgotten. The softer tones put listeners at ease and make them feel warm and relaxed. Ishii argues that the quality of CDs and today's speakers are so good, they simply reveal the limitations of poor recordings, especially older music. By contrast, antique radios hide defects nicely with their vague but warm sounds.

In March 2005, he opened And Up, but business at the store has hardly been booming. Plenty of customers drop by and love the sound, but few seem willing to buy the pricey antiques. "It is hardly successful as a business," Ishii shrugged.

3

4

7

8

FANS FORGE FUTURE iPODS

For a peek into the dark recesses of the iPod community's collective id, there's a gallery of iPod concept designs at the iLounge website. The extensive collection of Photoshop prototypes showcases more than 220 speculative designs of future iPods, created primarily by amateurs who wanted to share their wish lists of new iPod features or capabilities. In general, the work is high quality. The designs are incredibly detailed, beautifully rendered, and well thought out.

And what do these iPod fantasists want? Well, they want video, and they want a PDA. Oh dear. Apple Computer's CEO, Steve Jobs, has nixed both—for now. "We don't see a market for people that want to watch video on these portable devices," Jobs told the *Wall Street Journal*.

Applele hiSpeaker

If only Apple could find ways to bring the iLounge's concept designs to market, everyone would be happy. Video, battery life, and cost are no problem in fantasyland. Take for example, the iSpec video iPod, designed by Joe Kosinsky, director of New York design firm Kdlab.

Kosinsky's iSpec is a futuristic iPod shaped like a pair of Brad Pitt's sunglasses. Controlled by a finger-mounted splint, video is projected onto the interior of the glass lenses. Earbuds are built in. The iSpec features an immersive, 3-D interface reminiscent of Apple's experimental HotSauce Web interface developed in the mid-'90s. To illustrate his ideas, Kosinsky created an impressive video of the iSpec experience as a spec project (hence the name) for his portfolio. The video, created in Discreet's 3ds Max software, has proven a popular download—75,000 hits in the first month—and has sparked passionate debate on the Web, much to Kosinsky's surprise and delight. "A lot of people think it's real," he said. "They write to me and ask when it's going to come out.... (Others) get very angry. They think it's going in the wrong direction. They say it's a stupid idea: How can you walk and watch video at the same time? I think its great there's such emotions and passion about a fantasy product."

Indeed, many of the other concept designs elicit long strings of comments debating their pros and cons too. To Christian Schluender, general manager of Silicon Valley firm frog design, the designs and the debate are an elaborate form of worship. "[The iPod] is a beautiful product," he said. "The whole experience is extremely well thought out and designed, and people want this in other parts of their lives...in their phones and their DVD players.... It's a social statement. It's pretty interesting stuff."

Several of the product mock-ups blend the iPod with a phone. One nicely rendered hybrid, featuring a slide-out keypad, mixes a video player with a cell phone and a PDA. Judging by the concept designs, PDA functions are high on iPod wish lists. There's nothing some iPod fans would like more than to see a blend of iPod and Newton, the PDA Apple discontinued in 1998. The Newton is still widely mourned.

Japanese photographer Isamu Sanada, known for his Apple product mock-ups, contributed an iPod-cum-Newton wristwatch. Sanada's hiPod is a combo MP3 player/cell phone/PDA with a flip-up screen and wireless earbuds. The hiPod is a clever riff on design elements from Apple and Nokia. By combining the iPod's scroll wheel with Nokia's circular dial pad (found on phones such as the 3650), Sanada has dreamed up a nifty interface that looks like it might actually work. "He's good," said frog design's Schluender. "He's really captured the essence of Apple's products."

Another Sanada design also utilizes a slide-out PDA keypad. This is a full-on OS X iPod—a pocket iMac capable of running iTunes and iPod photo.

(FACING PAGE) Japanese photographer Isamu Sanada designed these good-looking iPod speakers. Sanada's design is clearly influenced by Apple's Power Mac G5 and iSight video camera. Too bad they're not real. CREDIT: ISAMU SANADA; (THIS PAGE) Designed by Joe Kosinsky, the iSpec is a futuristic iPod shaped like a pair of Brad Pitt's sunglasses. CREDIT: JOE KOSINSKY

1

2

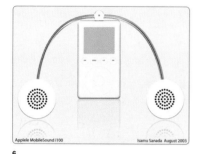

6

7

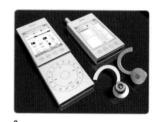

8

12

13

Shrinking the iPod in size is another popular idea; the mini becomes the micro. One iPod micro concept design shrinks the iPod to a key fob. The iPod has also been reimagined as a pen, with the screen and scroll wheel wrapping around the barrel. The button at the top of the pen acts as the "select" control. So far so good, but its creator also includes a built-in laser pointer, for some reason. "This tool is best for tricking around in exams or similar," its creator explains.

How about a handy iPod-cum-beverage cooler?

For MP3Js, there's the iPod Mixer, which fuses a pair of iPods into a pair of DJ's decks. Pitch, volume, and crossfade are all built in, allowing easy mixing, scratching, and beat matching.

Then there's cybernetics. The borgPod features the iPod's "sexy scroll wheel surgically implanted on the back of (the) hand." But should you try to play illegally downloaded songs on the borgPod, "You'll be greeted by Apple's new iToughlove software: a nervous-systemwide shock, and the mantra 'Don't Steal Music' repeated nonstop for seven days in a firm yet pleasing voice."

3

4

5

iPod - revolutions
Scroll-Wheel around the Stick
Select-Button on Top
Laserpointer
Bluetooth

9

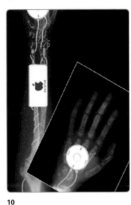

10

11

iPod X

16

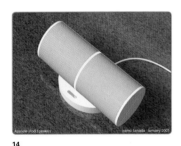
Applele iPod Speakers   Isamu Sanada   January 2005

14

iPod flash
Applele iPod flash R2   Isamu Sanada / February 2005

15

(1) A lot of iPod mock-ups blend the iPod and PDA, like this mini iPod-cum-cellphone. CREDIT: iLOUNGE; (2, 6, 8, 11, 12, 13, 14, 15) Japanese photographer Isamu Sanada's various iPod designs drew raves from professional industrial designers. "He's good," said Frog Design's Christian Schluender. "He's really captured the essence of Apple's products." CREDIT: ISAMU SANADA; (3) This iPod concept is shaped like Apple's distinctive logo. CREDIT: iLOUNGE; (4) Several mockups see the iPod shrunk to a wristwatch. CREDIT: iLOUNGE; (5) This circular iPod concept incorporates the scroll wheel controls into a round, touch-sensitive screen. CREDIT: iLOUNGE; (7) This concept iPod plays cool tunes while chilling drinks. CREDIT: iLOUNGE; (9) The iPod rejigged as a pen. CREDIT: iLOUNGE; (10) The borgPod features the iPod's "scroll wheel surgically implanted on the back of [the] hand." But should you try to play illegally downloaded songs on the borgPod, "You'll be greeted by Apple's new iToughlove software: a nervous-systemwide shock, and the mantra 'Don't Steal Music' repeated nonstop for seven days in a firm yet pleasing voice." CREDIT: iLOUNGE; (16) The iPod X is imagined as a portable music machine with attitude to spare: "With a press of a button … Bose speakers will come out from the sides and blast 300 watts of music into your drums." CREDIT: iLOUNGE

In 2005, New York saw a big jump in iPod robberies, according to news reports. By the end of March, there were 304 robberies in the city's transit system and 462 larcenies, up significantly from the year before, according to police. Although these weren't all acts of iTheft, police do attribute the general increase to the growing number of iPods getting snatched. **CREDIT:** LEANDER KAHNEY

Security in Obscurity

Photographer Symon Chow uses the NYC trains every day and doesn't like taking his iPod out of his pocket. So he had the clever idea of disguising it as a pack of cigarettes. Chow simply printed out a Camel-themed iPod skin and stuck it on his player. "I figured deception would be the best way to go," he wrote on Spymac. "No one is gonna give it a second look if at first glance they see a pack of cigarettes."

iPOD JACKING

During his regular evening walk, software executive Steve Crandall often nods a polite greeting to other iPod users he passes. It's easy to spot the distinctive white earbuds threaded from pocket to ears. Crandall, the 51-year-old CTO of Omenti Research, lives in Basking Ridge, New Jersey, a "nice, middle-class small town."

But while quietly enjoying some chamber music one evening in August, Crandall's polite nodding protocol was rudely shattered. Crandall was boldly approached by another iPod user, a 30ish woman bopping enthusiastically to some high-energy tune only she could hear. "She walked right up to me and got within my comfort field," Crandall stammered. "I was taken aback. She pulled out the earbuds on her iPod and indicated the jack with her eyes." Warily unplugging his own earbuds, Crandall gingerly plugged them into the woman's iPod and was greeted by a rush of techno.

"We listened for about 30 seconds," Crandall said. "No words were exchanged. We nodded and walked off."

The following evening, Crandall saw the woman again. This time, she was sharing her iPod with another iPod regular Crandall had spotted on his walks. Within a couple of days, Crandall had performed the iPod sharing ritual with all the four or five other regulars he sees on his walks. Since August, they've listened to each other's music dozens of times. "It's very strange," he said. "It's almost like you're being a DJ for the other person.... It's very gratifying if you see someone dancing around to the music you're listening to. It's a great feeling to see other people enjoying your music, and my tastes are fairly bizarre."

Crandall is into indigenous music from northern Europe, like the tribal folk music of the Sami. But he's been turned on to techno and other unfamiliar types of music he's heard on his acquaintances' iPods, especially the one owned by the 30ish woman. "She listens to techno and trance and things like that," he said. "Things I'm completely disconnected from. Stuff I'd never listen to unless someone is guiding me.... It's interesting. I've probably bought half a dozen CDs based on what I've heard. It's like finding a new radio station."

In fact, Crandall has taken to carrying pen and paper to jot down titles he likes. The others do the same. Generally, no one speaks, but "it's a very friendly sort of thing," Crandall said. "It's kind of nice to keep it very private."

This "iPod jacking," as Crandall calls it, appears to be a phenomenon restricted to Crandall and his iPod friends, though others have tried it. After posting a note about his experiences on his blog, Crandall received responses from several others who have shared their iPods with strangers. Crandall said he received reports that iPod jack sharing occurs at Oberlin College and is practiced in Cambridge in the United Kingdom, another college town.

"It's not widespread at all, but it's the kind of thing that might take off on a campus or in a small community," Crandall said. Crandall said he tried sharing iPods in New York's SoHo District with about six people he passed on the sidewalk. Three gave him dirty looks and moved on quickly, while the other three reciprocated. "I don't think it's a native activity there," he said.

Dennis Lloyd, publisher of the iLounge, said he was only aware of jack sharing through a thread started by Crandall on the site's forums. But he liked the idea. "With so many people plugged in these days, it's nice to hear people are actually connecting in the real world," he said. "Reach out and jack someone."

Author Douglas Rushkoff suggested that iPod sharing is a legacy of online file sharing—essentially the same thing, except offline. "It's kind of a stoner's ethic, really, the way you pass the joint at a Dead show," he said.

Sharing an iPod through its headphone jack is also a crude, low-tech version of what some predict is the real killer application of future iPods: transforming them into short-distance broadcasting devices by adding Bluetooth or similar radio technology, coupled with Bonjour, an Apple-developed networking technology that allows devices to discover each other automatically.

The prospect of letting iPod users listen to each other's libraries wirelessly has sparked numerous excited forum posts on the iLounge and other sites.

The Register's Andrew Orlowski, for example, has suggested several times that turning an iPod into a personal micro-radio station would be "revolutionary." "It would greatly annoy the RIAA [Recording Industry Association of America], which would argue that it's a portable Napster," he wrote in 2002. "But...this music-sharing appliance could have fairly dramatic social effects.... You could get promiscuous with strangers: You could pair and exchange a song on the same short bus ride. You could create short, ad hoc personal broadcasts, to anyone else with a Bluetooth iPod. You could have a 'What am I listening to?' menu option and share your choice with anyone within discoverable range."

Taking Orlowski's "what am I listening to?" option to its logical conclusion, others have suggested that files received wirelessly could be looked up automatically on Apple's iTunes Music Store when users plug their iPods into their main computer. Users would then be asked if they wanted to buy and download the tunes they heard on the road.

DANCING WITH COMMUTERS

In London, a new type of dance club has emerged. Instead of going to a noisy club, revelers are gathering in public places to dance to the sound of their own portable music players. "At 6.58pm precisely, dozens of individuals dotted around the concourse at Victoria station, each wearing headphones, begin to dance," reported the London's *Independent*. "Lost in their private musical world, they all bop happily on the spot to their heart's content. Welcome to the world of mobile clubbing, the latest underground, and somewhat surreal, movement taking hold in the capital." "It was like re-visiting the trauma of a school disco," said one reviewer of a mobile club at London Bridge Station.

iPODS BEAT IN HEART OF THE CITY

Search for the word *iPod* on New York's craigslist classified ads website, and you open a strange window into the psyche of the city. Naturally, an eye-opening search isn't conducted in the For Sale section, which simply displays a pedestrian list of iPods available for purchase. A truly illuminating search must include the personal ads, which offer some insight into the culture of iPods but reveal even more about the city's personality.

In March 2004, for example, a boy from Brooklyn wanted advice about his girlfriend, who had dismissed his gift of an expensive handbag. She wanted an iPod mini instead. According to the boy's report, the girlfriend complained the bag was good only for a single season, and besides, if they broke up, she'd have the iPod to remember him by. "Like should I dump her because this is just one more reason why I feel we can't be together?" he wrote in the craigslist post asking for advice. Alas, the advice he received wasn't much help. Someone recommended dumping the girl and selling the bag on eBay.

And then there was the guy who needed an imaginary girlfriend for an evening while his parents visited from out of town. He'd lied to them about having a girlfriend, and he needed a pretend mate for a dinner date. In return for feigned love, he'd buy her an iPod. However, the ad insisted the lucky girl have a great butt and legs, which raised suspicions that the poster's intentions might not have been as honorable as he proclaimed. The ad was quickly pulled off the site. Nonetheless, the poster received 30 or 40 emails from willing imaginary girlfriends, he said in response to an email inquiry. "I got an amazing response," he said. "Everyone is overjoyed with my concept, although several of these girls asked if I could give them new shoes instead of an iPod." He didn't respond to subsequent emails asking how the charade played out.

A mobile club outside London's Euston train station. Revelers gather to dance without speakers or music. The soundtrack is supplied by each person's personal music player. CREDIT: PETER BURNETT

In a similar vein, there are several ads offering certain "services" in exchange for an iPod. With admirable economy, a young gay man says simply that he'll perform oral sex for an iPod. A cute 19-year-old says, "I need $100 to buy an iPod and I'm horny. Simple as that." College girl Chloe makes a similar offer because she has bills to pay. "I bought lots of clothes, an iPod, and other things and charged it to my credit card," she says. "I don't want my dad to know."

Many of the personal ads are "missed connections"—lonely hearts trying to connect with the attractive stranger they saw on the subway or a coffee shop. "Where are you my iPod man?" asks the tall Asian girl with glasses seeking a 6-foot-tall Hispanic male. "I asked you about your iPod with the blue cover, and you just went on ranting about how iPod is the invention of the century," she writes. "You did not notice I was looking into your hazel eyes!"

Being personal ads, several people use the iPod as a way to advertise their tastes or lifestyle. An older fashionista seeking young hipster boy says her ideal toyboy wears a blazer, white T-shirt, and "prerequisite" iPod. He's got to have money, she says, and, presumably, a dictionary. On the other hand, a tall, lean hipster looking for a casual encounter boasts he'd never be seen with an iPod "stuck to my head."

For some reason, the personals also feature an ongoing discussion of the *meaning* of the iPod on New York's streets, especially the signature white earphone wires, which some feel are "showy." "I have no problem with anyone using the iPod. What does bother me is people who continue to wear the white earbuds," complains one. "They suck, but they (wear) them so other people would know they have an iPod. We should sell the earbuds without iPods so people can make others think they have an iPod when in reality, it's attached to, say, nothing. But hey, they will look cool."

Others say the sight of white wires makes them curious about the wearer. "Makes me question their income, housing, their career choice, educational background, political and social affiliations, and all kinds of crap," says one poster.

It should be noted that similar searches on craigslist in San Francisco, Los Angeles, and London fail to return anywhere near the volume of posts or anything like the same results. The only posts of note occur in California, where hitchhikers looking for rides promise to bring an iPod and "take care of the tunes."

II Now Playing ▰▰▰

7 of 8

Spend, Spend, Spend
(on iPod Accessories)

0:00   -4:04

MENU

One of the unique things about the iPod is how much owners spend on accessories. The electronics industry has a rule of thumb that gadget owners spend about 10 percent of a device's cost on extras to trick it out, according to CNET News.com. But with the iPod, owners are spending a lot more, in many cases as much again as the iPod itself, sometimes more. And, according to Apple's iPod product manager, Danika Cleary, the company's research shows that every single person who buys an iPod also buys at least one accessory.

David Glickman, a San Francisco management consultant, bought an iPod in 2003 and then splashed out on "noise-canceling headphones, mini-speakers from Sony, an FM radio transmitter, adapters for charging in cars, a cable to connect the player to his stereo, and an adapter so he and a family member can listen simultaneously,: according to *Businessweek*.

As the iPod takes off, the market for accessories is becoming very, very big. In the early years, only a handful of tiny firms eked a living from rubber cases and auto chargers. "There's an incredible iPod economy out there," said Apple CEO Steve Jobs at the Macworld Expo in January 2005. "There are now over 400 accessory products you can get for your iPod. This is unmatched in the industry by a mile."

Accessories for the iPod range from $10 silicon rubber cases to $4,500 tube amps. There are also chargers, speakers, cables, FM transmitters, robot-shaped docks, and even the $149 iBoom, which turns the iPod into a boom box. For one of the latest iPod models, the shuffle, Apple introduced a half-dozen add-ons, including a hard case, a battery pack, and an armband for wearing the device while working out.

One of the hottest development areas is products that connect the iPod to the car—the environment in which a third of music listening takes place. Several carmakers are adding iPod connectors to their vehicles as factory options, including such high-end names such as Alfa Romeo, BMW, Ferrari, Mercedes-Benz, Nissan, and Volvo. "Now you can get anything from a red plastic case for a few dollars, to a red Ferrari for a few hundred thousand," Apple's head of marketing, Phil Schiller, joked to *Businessweek*.

Apple introduced a Made for iPod program, which awards a warranty seal to technical products authorized by the company. The program extracts a licensing fee—a small one, according to Apple. As well as accessories, the iPod has also inspired a range of new music-related services, such as companies that will load a customer's iPod with music for them and another that develops playlists intended for doctors to listen to while performing surgery.

AS THE iPOD TAKES OFF, THE MARKET FOR ACCESSORIES IS BECOMING VERY VERY

Tim Hickman rode the dot-com roller coaster and emerged with a new company, Speck Products, which makes a popular case for the iPod. The Flip-Stand is a hard case with a flip-down scroll wheel protector that turns the case into a desktop stand. It was a big hit at Macworld; Hickman sold out his entire stock. "They were flown into the country on Monday, we announced them on Tuesday, and they were sold out on Thursday," he said proudly. "We've got 50 more being driven up from Palo Alto. They should be here any second. We're off to the races." **CREDIT:** LEANDER KAHNEY

Paul Griffin, CEO of Griffin Technology (www. griffintechnology.com), is rightly proud of his company's iTrip, an FM transmitter for the iPod. The little gizmo has helped make Griffin Technology one of the hottest iPod accessory makers on the market. The iTrip sits atop the iPod and allows songs to be transmitted to any nearby FM tuner, such as a car stereo. Griffin said it draws no more power than a pair of headphones and can be tuned to any frequency. "It's the coolest accessory for the iPod right now," he beamed. "Until someone comes up with something better, that is," he added, laughing. **CREDIT:** LEANDER KAHNEY

SERVICE TURNS CDs INTO MP3s

Nova Spivack, a well-heeled New Yorker and technophile, had been dying to get an iPod for a long time. The problem wasn't money; it was Spivack's giant CD collection. He couldn't face the chore of converting 1,000-plus CDs to digital format. Then Spivack, the CEO of Radar Networks, discovered RipDigital, a firm that offers a simple but labor-saving service. For about a dollar a disc, the company converts entire CD collections to MP3 files, all nicely organized by artist and album.

Spivack boxed up his CDs and shipped them to RipDigital. Four days later he got them back, along with an external hard drive containing MP3s of his entire CD collection. "It's really changed my listening experience," Spivack said. "The nice thing about digital is it reminds you what you have, instead of it sitting in a case on your wall. I made a bunch of playlists, and I'm listening to music all the time again."

It may seem odd that a company could turn a profit by performing a task that anyone can do himself. But RipDigital—and a half-dozen companies like it—know that, for some people, time is more valuable than money. "I got my whole collection on my PC in about half an hour, instead of a month," Spivack said. Spivack isn't looking back. Having digitized his collection, Spivack tossed all the extraneous CD cases in the trash. He's keeping the original discs as backup only.

Dick Adams, one of RipDigital's three cofounders, said the service has been growing in popularity since its launch in December 2004. "We've been overwhelmed with orders and scrambling to keep up," he said. "It's been fabulous." Adams said the company initially targeted DJs, radio stations, and institutions such as hotels and libraries. Adams said they hoped to entice serious audiophiles and collectors but were surprised by the reaction from regular consumers. "There are a lot of people out there who have more money than time," said Adams. "Most people don't roll their own cigarettes, and a lot of people don't want to do this themselves."

After receiving an order, RipDigital sends customers a box with spindles for their CDs (the jewel cases aren't shipped) and a shipping label. Customers load the spindles with their CDs and ship the package to RipDigital; about a week later, they get their discs back, along with DVDs containing their songs in high-fidelity MP3 format. If they prefer, songs can be loaded onto an external hard drive.

"The quality is good," said Neal Howard, a professional DJ from Atlanta, who is using the company to steadily digitize his collection of several hundred CDs.

Though RipDigital uses MP3 format by default, the company will rip songs using any codec the customer wants—Microsoft's WMA or Apple's AAC, for example. Adams said so far, the WMA/AAC split has been about 50/50. The ripping process is highly automated, although Adams declined to go into detail for "competitive reasons." He said each CD is ripped individually and the files erased after they are dispatched to the customer. The company does not keep a library of files it has ripped, Adams said. RipDigital marks each song with a digital watermark, which can identify each client. Adams said the watermark acts as insurance should customers start loading songs onto file-sharing networks. The company does not use the information and has no plans to do so, Adams said.

Joe Wilcox, a senior analyst at Jupiter Research, said he was surprised that people would pay for a service like this. He said he ripped his CD collection himself. "It's not that painful," he said. Wilcox also doubted that CDs are doomed. Jupiter's studies predict that for the next several years the percentage of people downloading music will remain in single digits, compared with the number of CD buyers, Wilcox said. "Our data shows that CDs are going to be around for a long time," he said. "MP3s and other digital formats are still in their infancy."

But for Spivack, the CD is a thing of the past. "I've become a total iPod fanatic," he said. "In the week since I've got this, I've spent about $500 at the Apple Music Store. My productivity is going down. Now all I do is play with digital music."

iPOD MUZAK ISN'T SAME OLD SONG

Music entrepreneurs are using Apple's iPod to put a new spin on old-fashioned Muzak. Instead of piping bland background music over tinny speakers, enterprising music promoters are loading hundreds of hours of hip tunes onto iPods and renting them to restaurants, nightspots, clothing boutiques, and hair salons.

"It's hard for (smaller independent) labels to get exposure, and it's hard for stores to get the right music," said Lara Wiesenthal, the brains behind an iPod music service called Activaire. "I really get the perfect music into the stores, and it allows me to disseminate the labels' music to a different audience." Wiesenthal, a 33-year-old architect, runs Activaire part time with her husband, Adesh Deosaran, and a couple of partners. Based in New York, Wiesenthal calls Activaire a "music stylist." The service provides music to a half-dozen boutiques and jewelers in New York, Paris, and California. For $100 a month, Wiesenthal's clients rent an iPod with about 30 hours of music handpicked to suit their business environment.

(RIGHT) Nova Spivack can now toss out his 1,000-plus jewel cases and CDs after converting them all to MP3s using RipDigital's service. CREDIT: COURTESY OF NOVA SPIVACK/FEATURE PHOTO SERVICE; (BOTTOM) The Activaire crew, records, laptops, and iPods. CREDIT: ACTIVAIRE

Activaire is also working with several hotels to design their music experience, including Hotel Victor in Miami's trendy South Beach and KSL resorts. Guests rent or buy the iPods, which can be plugged into Bose Sound Docks in their rooms or scattered around the resort. "Hotels are all about environment and the user experience, so it's a wonderful contract," said Wiesenthal.

Activaire offers personalized music collections to individual consumers as well. Each week, Activaire picks the top 10 albums in its rotation. Subscribers to Personal Activaire get these albums loaded onto their iPods and can visit a customized private online account to view artwork from the albums and information about the artists. It's like having a friend who makes you mix tapes, except you pay them.

Wiesenthal has licensed hundreds of songs from nearly 100 independent labels, most specializing in cutting-edge electronica. From her library of hundreds of gigabytes of songs, Wiesenthal can tailor about 30 hours of music for each client. "The point is to provide the stores with more music than they were used to, and to make it automatic, hands-off," she said. "The iPod makes it really easy. They can even hit different playlists for different moods—one for the morning, the afternoon, or evening."

Every three months, Wiesenthal ships a new iPod to her clients with a new selection of music. The clients return the old iPod via a package delivery service.

"It's like Muzak, I guess, but I don't consider them competition," Wiesenthal said. Muzak, the biggest of several music providers in the United States, has become virtually synonymous with the background music played in supermarkets, malls, and elevators the world over. In 2004, Muzak reported first quarter revenues of $60 million. But it's targeting a very different audience. "Electronica is not the kind of music they use," explained Wiesenthal. "A company like Muzak would never license from the labels I license from."

Another popular service, Baby Activaire, is a package for new parents that includes a pink or blue iPod mini, a Bose Sound Dock, and a dozen mixes with names such as "Chill," "Loungey Lullabies," and "Energized Play Tunes."

There's also Surgical Activaire—an iPod designed to help surgeons perform operations. "Many surgeons are carrying and using iPods now," said Wiesenthal. "The surgical playlist is being developed in conjunction with Dr. Sotiris Stamou, a Washington, DC, heart specialist, specifically for a coronary bypass. Each surgery is unique, and the iPod's playlist feature allows us to style music for the various aspects of surgery."

On Valentine's Day, Activaire offered an iHeart iPod, preloaded with "a musical love potion brewed by the company's music stylists."

Wiesenthal doesn't yet make a living from Activaire, but she would dearly love to. She exudes missionary zeal. "I love doing this," she said. "My goal is to expose the mainstream to electronic music. I'm very positive about it because there's so much great stuff available. I think it'll take off. We've got some really exciting things coming up."

In Philadelphia, Adam Porter, a 29-year-old DJ and owner of Cue Records, an independent record store, hit on an idea similar to Wiesenthal's. Like Wiesenthal, Porter sends out iPods loaded with music from his store's extensive catalog. He has clients at about a half-dozen restaurants, lounges, and hair salons around Philadelphia. "I'm trying to expose independent artists and acts and generate more revenue for my music store," he said. "This is a great way to do that. They get the flexibility of a DJ without the DJ ego and attitude."

Unlike Wiesenthal, Porter hasn't started charging for his services. He's unsure about the legality of renting copyright music. He hopes he's covered by the ASCAP (American Society of Composers, Authors and Publishers) licensing fees his clients already pay for music played at their establishments, but he's hesitant to start charging until he's consulted a lawyer. Still, Porter said the service isn't about money. "I'm trying to expose people to good music," he said. "I'm trying to find a way to market good music when there's a void of good radio here in Philadelphia."

One of Porter's nonpaying clients, Roger Main, general manager of the Adriatica restaurant/lounge, said he's delighted with the service. "I'm a technophobe. I didn't know how it was going to take care of us," Main said. "But it does a great job. The bartender chooses the playlist. It's better than a jukebox. The establishment controls the mood, not the customers."

Porter said he's been trying to find a way to market independent music for years. He experimented with mix tapes and custom CDs, but was never able to provide the variety and convenience that comes with using an iPod. "When the iPod came along, it was so easy, it was beautiful," he said. "You edit out all the bad stuff, all the filler songs, and you give people beautiful music. There's an endless supply, and it's always cutting edge and hip and cool."

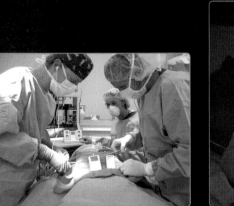

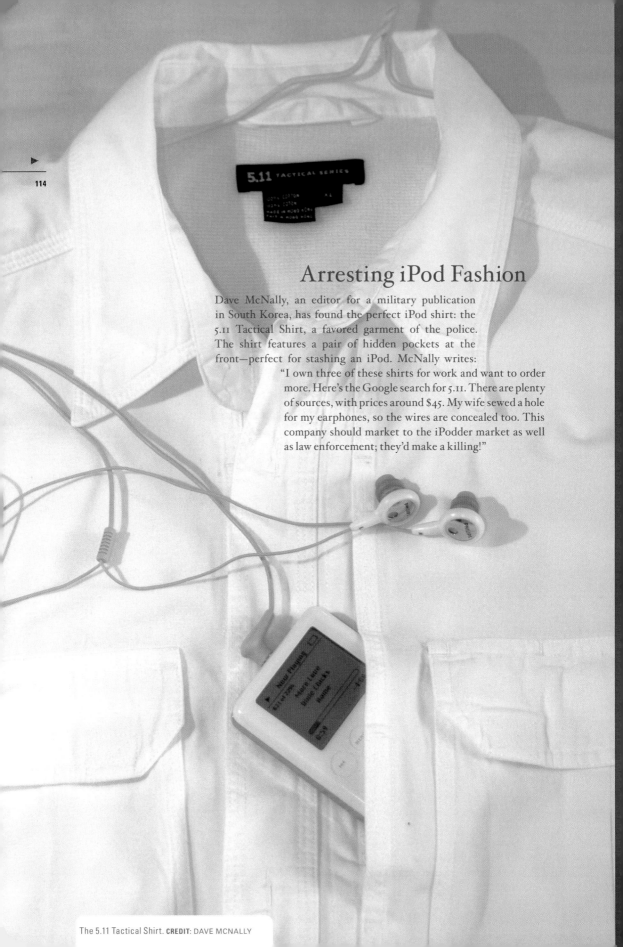

Arresting iPod Fashion

Dave McNally, an editor for a military publication in South Korea, has found the perfect iPod shirt: the 5.11 Tactical Shirt, a favored garment of the police. The shirt features a pair of hidden pockets at the front—perfect for stashing an iPod. McNally writes:

"I own three of these shirts for work and want to order more. Here's the Google search for 5.11. There are plenty of sources, with prices around $45. My wife sewed a hole for my earphones, so the wires are concealed too. This company should market to the iPodder market as well as law enforcement; they'd make a killing!"

The 5.11 Tactical Shirt. **CREDIT**: DAVE MCNALLY

TEMPEST IN A SPECIALTY iPOD CASE

With all the affection lavished on iPods, it's saddening to discover how the lovable device destroyed a friendship. Two entrepreneurs on separate continents are locked in mortal combat for a lucrative piece of turf—the market for rubbery iPod accessories.

Since 2003, Andrew Ackloo of iSkin and Lajo Cymbalski of Xskn have been feuding over the sale and distribution of silicon rubber iPod cases. The former friends and business partners now head separate companies making similar products with similar names. The two have traded threats and insults in letters to business partners and in public forums and have pressured distributors to drop the other's products. "In the beginning it was brutal," said a friend of one of the partners, who asked not to be identified. "The only reason they got up in the morning was to put each other out of business."

The pair went into business together in 2002, producing silicon rubber cases for Apple's iPod called eXo skin, which were sold under the iSkin brand. Ackloo said he and Cymbalski had a verbal agreement. Ackloo designed and marketed the cases, while Cymbalski, who lives in China, took care of the manufacturing. But in late 2003, as Ackloo prepared to launch a new iSkin product called the eXo 2, Cymbalski began selling his own eXo 2 case under his own Lajo brand. "We were friends," said Ackloo, but "greed got the better of him."

Despite several attempts, Cymbalski couldn't be reached for comment. However, Cymbalski claims *he* designed all the cases and that iSkin acted merely as a reseller, according to a statement on the iLounge forums, purportedly taken from an email written by Cymbalski.

One distributor of iPod accessories, who sells both companies' products, said the dispute was rancorous. The source said iSkin threatened to pull its products if he continued to sell Cymbalski's Xskn cases. "They didn't like us selling his stuff," the source said. "The iSkin guys are really trying to put him out."

The two companies continue to sell similar products with similar names. Cymbalski's Xskn sells a line of eXo cases, while iSkin markets eVo cases. Whatever the nomenclature, business appears to be good. iSkin held a product launch party at Justin's, P. Diddy's upscale New York restaurant. "I'm not going to say Lajo is a bad guy," Ackloo said. "Business is business.... It's unfortunate, but that's what happened."

(ABOVE) iSkin's case provides a protective skin for Apple's iPod.
CREDIT: COURTESY OF iSKIN

After his iPod photo was squeezed to death on a packed commuter train, an unnamed Japanese tinkerer created his own armored iPod carrying case. According to a Google translation of his website, the crush of commuters cracked the iPod's screen and put a big dent in the rear.

"Pressure of that horrible commuter train has been experienced," he wrote. Apparently, the car's handrail was positioned at the exact height where he carried his iPod, and there it was no contest when the two collided. To prevent this from happening again, the commuter made an armored case from hefty plates of machined aluminum and some bolts. So strong is the case, its maker reckoned it could stop a bullet from a handgun.

A ONE-STOP SHOP FOR iPOD ADD-ONS

iLOUNGE DRUNK WITH SUCCESS

In the world of iPods, it's not just the makers of rubbery prophylactic cases who are blossoming. The burgeoning market for iPod news and reviews has propelled a scrappy one-man website into the big dog of online iPod publishers. In recent months, iLounge has grown from a niche website into a professional publishing operation with big plans. Riding the wave of iPod popularity, the site is a daily read for an ever-growing army of fans. Unique visitors doubled to 2 million a month in early 2005, and about 1,000 new members are joining its online forums every month. To cope with the load, the website doubled its server capacity and trebled its staff—to a total of three.

Known for its near-comprehensive library of reviews—almost every iPod case and accessory undergoes exhaustive evaluation—the site is a one-stop shop for iPod add-ons. And its recently expanded news operation is helping iLounge become a source of authoritative comment on all things iPod, with quotes in the *New York Times* and the *Wall Street Journal*.

Dennis Lloyd, a web designer from Irvine, California, launched the site in late 2001, just a couple of weeks after Apple introduced the iPod. Shortly after starting the site, Lloyd became unemployed. "I turned it into a full-time job because I got laid off," said Lloyd. "I was just sitting at home collecting unemployment. I had this site, so I started working on it every day."While doing contract work, Lloyd attracted his first advertiser in spring 2002. By mid-2003, he had enough ads to support himself, and in 2004, ads were bringing in enough revenue to expand the site and hire two full-time employees.

Jeremy Horwitz, the editor-in-chief who writes most of the reviews, was working as an intellectual property lawyer before he was hired. Larry Angell, the news editor, was lured away from MacMinute, one of the best Mac news sites on the Web.

"They are in the enviable position of being in the right place at the right time," said Andrew Green, vice president of marketing at Digital Lifestyle Outfitters, one of iLounge's first advertisers. "They're the go-to guys." Green said, in terms of iPod-related traffic, the site is bested only by Apple.com. In addition, iLounge isn't hampered by ties to the more established Mac publishing industry. In other words, it's an advertiser's dream. "Eighty percent of iPod users are on Windows," Green said. "Playing to the Mac audience (such as *Macworld* magazine readers) misses 80 percent of the potential market."

UPPER CASE

The iPod has become as ubiquitous in 2004 as the boom box was during the '80s. So how to **distinguish yourself** from the rest of the pack? Choose a cover that reflects your singular style.

118

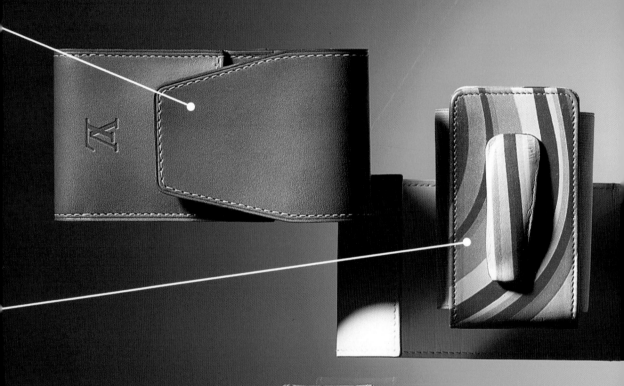

ll make a bold statement every
ard leather panels keep your
lastic sides keep it snug. Be
hat you like — your iPod's not

Must-Haves for the Upper West Side

In the 2004 fall fashion issue, New York's trendy *City* magazine printed a roundup of designer iPod cases. The spread featured creations from Louis Vuitton, Dior, Gucci, Paul Smith, and Dunhill. "The iPod has become as ubiquitous in 2004 as the boom box was during the '80s," the magazine said. "So how to distinguish yourself from the rest of the pack? Choose a cover that reflects your singular style."

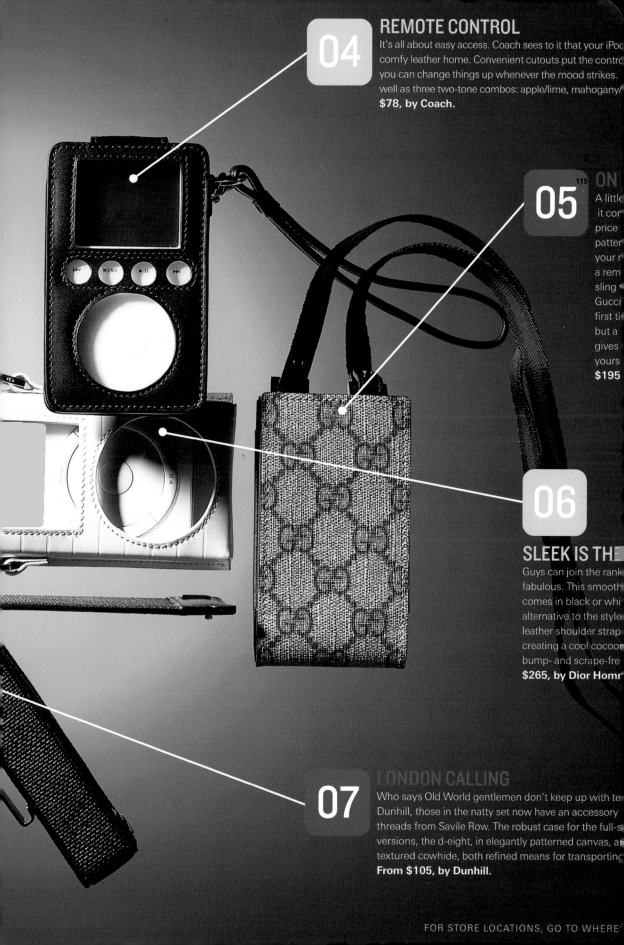

REMOTE CONTROL

04

It's all about easy access. Coach sees to it that your iPod
comfy leather home. Convenient cutouts put the contro
you can change things up whenever the mood strikes.
well as three two-tone combos: apple/lime, mahogany/
$78, by Coach.

ON

05 [119]

A little
it cor
price
patter
your r
a rem
sling
Gucci
first ti
but a
gives
yours
$195

06

SLEEK IS THE

Guys can join the rank
fabulous. This smooth
comes in black or whi
alternative to the style
leather shoulder strap
creating a cool cocoo
bump- and scrape-fre
$265, by Dior Homr

LONDON CALLING

07

Who says Old World gentlemen don't keep up with te
Dunhill, those in the natty set now have an accessory
threads from Savile Row. The robust case for the full-s
versions, the d-eight, in elegantly patterned canvas, a
textured cowhide, both refined means for transportin
From $105, by Dunhill.

iPod Tube Amp Pumps Up the Price

Goldster Audio's Concertino tube amp and speaker system must be the priciest iPod accessory on the market. At $4,300, it's three times more expensive than Karl Lagerfeld's Jukebox bag. Still, there's nothing like the rich tone of tubes to warm the sound of badly encoded MP3s.

As the company proclaims, "...nothing compares to the unique and charming spectrum of tone colours of tube-based audio equipment. Once you get used to the richness of tone of a tube amplifier, you will disdain the synthetic, cool sound of a transistor for the rest of your life."

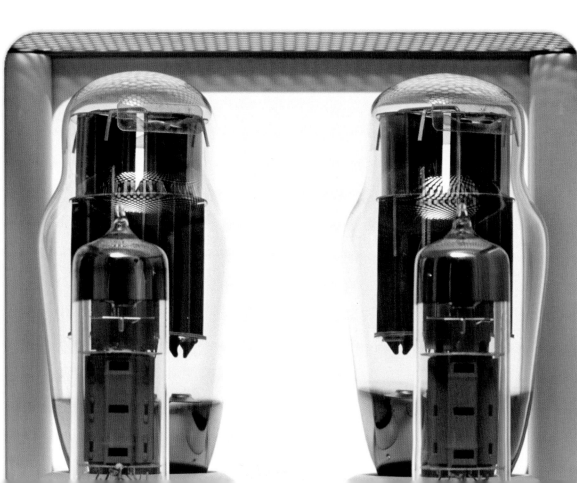

Framed iPod Speakers

The painting on the wall is actually an arty iPod speaker from Texas designer H. Michael Karshis. "[The artwork is] one in a series of my digital collage pieces consisting of some of my illustration, photography, and found art," he said. "There is also a five-inch speaker imbedded behind the nine chrome holes so you can hook up and listen to your iPod."

CREDIT: H. MICHAEL KARSHIS

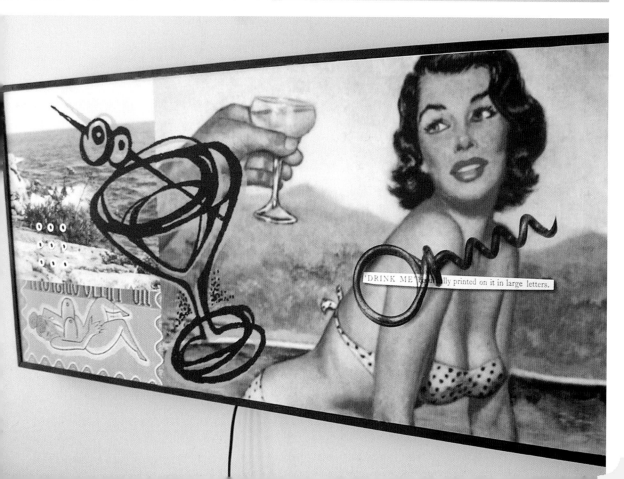

MAKING FREE iPODS PAY OFF

Unless you're extremely gullible, the promise of getting a free iPod from FreeiPods.com looks extremely dubious. But surprisingly, the site is legitimate. Lots of happy customers are popping up all over the Internet brandishing new iPods.

The program isn't a dodgy pyramid scheme; it's a new form of online marketing supported by companies such as eBay, AOL, and Columbia House. Here's how it works. FreeiPods.com promises an iPod or a $250 gift certificate to anyone who signs up for various online promotions and persuades five other people to participate. Subscribers are given a choice of 10 offers, including trials from big companies such as AOL or RealNetworks. Typically, the offers are free and easily canceled, although some require a credit card number. Once the trials are over—for both the main subscriber and all the people they refer—the free iPod is dispatched.

"Of course I was skeptical, but I didn't see any harm in trying," said Collin Grady, 22, from Salem, Oregon, who received his free iPod earlier this month and wrote about it on his blog. "All in all, a very painless process."

Indeed, some customers are so delighted that they've set up affiliate websites, called "conga lines," to persuade others the program isn't a swindle. "So many people on the Web think FreeiPods.com is a scam; I just wanted to prove them wrong," said John Sauer, a 19-year-old student at Boston's Berklee College of Music, who runs a different website called FreeiPodsandFlatScreens.com.

FreeiPods is one of several websites run by Gratis Internet, a Washington, DC, "customer acquisition" company owned by Peter Martin and Rob Jewell.

"I can definitely understand the skepticism," said Martin. "A lot of people believe there's no free lunch, but it's definitely not a scam. It's 100 percent legitimate."

We're shipping (iPods) every day." In a joint interview, Martin and Jewell denied that the site is a pyramid scheme, like the myriad matrix schemes advertised on eBay, which also promise free iPods. Instead, they explained, Gratis Internet receives a bounty for sending potential customers to sites such as AOL, eBay, or RealNetworks.

"We're a marketing firm," said Jewell. "We're sending these people to our advertisers. We cringe when we hear 'pyramid' or 'scheme.' We're more closely associated with viral marketing, with the subservient chicken, than Amway."

They declined to specify the bounty and said that the firm doesn't deal directly with the companies involved. Rather, Gratis Internet is commissioned by third-party marketing agencies, such as San Francisco's Adteractive.

Diego Canoso, Adteractive's vice president of sales, said FreeiPods.com is a lawful and well-run customer-acquisition program. "We've been working with these guys for more than three years," said Canoso. "They are very good at what they do."

Canoso also declined to specify the advertisers' bounties, but said they can range between $25 and $90 per referral, depending on the program and the kind of customer it attracts. "The money we give these guys (Gratis Internet) is enough to fulfill the promise that the customers come in for," Canoso said. Although $90 seems like a lot, Canoso said, it's peanuts compared with the millions spent on TV and magazine ads, which don't guarantee new customers. "Companies such as Columbia House (and) credit card companies, they're happy to pay for customers," Canoso said. "They're happy to send out iPods because they're getting customers in return. Capture is expensive, and they're paying after they've acquired the customer."

And although a lot of customers cancel after the free trial, enough stick around to make it worthwhile, Canoso said. Canoso also said that FreeiPods.com is at the forefront of performance-based marketing. "The model is beautiful," he said. "[The companies] are paying for a specific customer after acquiring the customer. It's not branding. It's not nonresponsive advertising.... It's low-risk marketing. It's a very efficient system."

For the last four years, Gratis Internet has operated customer-acquisition programs through FreeCDs.com, FreeDVDs.com, FreeVideoGames.com, and FreeCondoms.com. The company has sent out millions of dollars worth of free merchandise, Martin said, including 5 million to 6 million condoms. But nothing has taken off like the iPod offer. Between the launch of FreeiPods.com in June 2004 and March 2005, the company claims to have dispatched more than 11,000 iPods, worth more than $3.5 million.

iPOD SPAM AND SCAMS

The popularity of the iPod has spawned another kind of iPodtrepreneur: the crooked kind. The word *iPod*, for example, has become the most popular term in spam email, according to a 2005 report in Australia's *PC Authority* magazine. "Pushing aside usual spam categories, the iPod spam trimmed weight-loss spam to a svelte 3.6 percent of all spam sent in December," the magazine said. "Libido enhancement spam was rock solid at 35 percent, while sexual organ enhancement spam limped in at an unimpressive 3.6 percent of all spam sent."

Meanwhile, a search for *iPod* on eBay yields a couple thousand listings for the digital music player and accessories, but beware: hundreds of the listings are inducements to join pyramid-style scams. eBay is swamped with new "matrix" schemes, which appear to be legitimate buyers clubs but are in fact variations on classic pyramid scams, which are outlawed around the world. In most cases, eBay shoppers are offered hot products such as an iPod, a game console, or a cell phone at an incredible discount, say for $40 or $25. The eager bargain hunter is told not to bid on the item, but is directed instead to sites such as My3Mobile, The Phone Matrix, or Goraks.com, which offer iPods or cell phones as free gifts when products such as CDs or eBooks are purchased.

The catch is that buyers only get their free iPods after more people sign up. When making a purchase, the buyer's name is added to a list. As new members join, names are shuffled up the list. When they reach the top, the iPod is dispatched. To speed up the process, buyers are often encouraged to recruit new members to join the scheme. And that's where all the eBay posts come from. Victims are using eBay to recruit new members.

eBay spokesperson Hani Durzy said he was unaware of the scams. "We have 20 million items on the site at any one time. In the grand scheme of things, it is insignificant," Durzy said, referring to the large number of matrix listings on eBay.

In fact, matrix schemes are so common on eBay, some buyers think their ubiquity is a sign of legitimacy. "There are so many, you think there must be something to it," said Danny Yi, a 22-year-old graphic designer from New York, who signed up at My3Mobile for a free iPod with a $40 CD purchase. Recruited by an eBay listing, Yi said he bought a $40 CD at My3Mobile one week before posting his own iPod ads on eBay. Yi has yet to receive his CD or his iPod. Yi was surprised when told he was involved in a scam. "It seemed like something was not right," he said. "I was pretty skeptical. I'm still skeptical. But it's just $40, so I thought, why not? If you get it, great, but if not, so what? You learn your lesson."

James Kohm, an attorney with the Federal Trade Commission, which polices consumer scams, said he hadn't heard of matrix schemes, but if they worked as described, they are outlawed. "If that's what's going on," he said, "it's definitely illegal. You are always going to have more people who are not getting anything than those who are. Everybody's recruiting, but not everyone's going to get an iPod."

(THIS PAGE) Graphic designer Danny Yi's advertisement on eBay for a $40 iPod. Yi's eBay post is not an auction, but an attempt to recruit buyers for My3Mobile, which promises a free iPod with purchases. Trouble is, the iPod is dispatched only after several more people spend money at the site, hence Yi's ad for new recruits. The FTC says it's a classic pyramid scheme. **(FACING PAGE)** Here's the list of hopeful bargain hunters at My3Mobile who have signed up for a free iPod. As new members join the scheme, the person at the top of the list gets a free iPod, the site claims. The FTC says it's unlikely.

My3Mobile
mobile phone community

www.my3mobile.com

1 Buy a Mobile CD-ROM
2 Choose your FREE Gift
3 Enter My3Mobile Free Gift List

Home :: How It Works :: Products :: Free Gifts :: My3Mobile Lists :: Order Now :: FAQ :: Testimonials :: Forums :: Terms

My3Mobile Community JOIN NOW! | Mobile CD-ROM ORDER NOW! | Available Gifts CHECK IT OUT! | FREE Gifts! MY3MOBILE LISTS

Apple iPod (20GB) List

Currently waiting member: Stephen Dunthorne (steve73)
When the list below gets full, the next mobile is sent out.

Number of new members needed	Member name
1	Stephen Dunthorne (steve73)
2	Akber Ali Manji (manjidude) 2
3	ricci carlo (el.ricci)
4	filippo ferrer (Fish842001)
5	Prabhakar Chelliah (shadow4xp)
6	kurt hargreaves (kurthargreaves_5)
7	Ka Lap (pandamunky)
8	Mark Burns (monsterofart)
9	Tariq Alam (sarah_rizvi)
10	Charalambos (apoeld)
11	Jack Wang

The table below shows the list of members requesting this item.
The member in red will receive his/her iPod next.

Date	Name
26/01/2004	Stephen Dunthorne (steve73)
26/01/2004	Akber Ali Manji (manjidude) 2
26/01/2004	ricci carlo (el.ricci)
26/01/2004	filippo ferrer (Fish842001)
26/01/2004	Prabhakar Chelliah (shadow4xp)

II   Now Playing

8 of 8

I Want to Hold Your Handheld: Cultural Impact

0:00   -3:38

MENU

A good way to judge a person's character is by taking a peek at their music collection. As novelist Nick Hornby put it in *High Fidelity*: "It's no good pretending that any relationship has a future if your record collections disagree violently or if your favorite films wouldn't even speak to each other if they met at a party."

Now, thanks to the iPod and iTunes, there are new ways for people to look at one another's music collections. It's easy to browse someone's iPod to see what they like—if they'll show you, of course. And, thanks to iTunes' ability to share music collections over local networks, it's possible to judge someone's taste in music—or lack thereof—in a way that previously required a certain level of intimacy. The ability to examine the music collections of coworkers, neighbors, or fellow students is akin to peering into their true hidden souls. Someone who appears cool and with it from the outside could be revealed as a cultural nincompoop through the poor sap's atrocious taste in music.

And now that iTunes is becoming widely used on the PC platform, as well as the Mac, it is emerging that there are social implications for sharing music. On college campuses, for example, a new form of bigotry called "playlistism" is taking root. Invented by students at Wesleyan University, playlistism was first reported by Stephen Aubrey, a 20-year-old student and columnist for the *Wesleyan Argus*. Playlistism, Aubrey explained, is discrimination based not on race, sex, or religion, but on someone's terrible taste in music, as revealed by their iTunes music library.

Aubrey said an iTunes music library tells a lot more about a person than the clothes they wear or the books they carry. "It's the T-shirt, plus the book, plus the haircut," Aubrey said. "It's everything." Aubrey said Wesleyan students are enjoying a new parlor game—going through music libraries trying to guess what their owners are like. At any one time, dozens of iTunes libraries are available on the campus network, which is shared by about 2,000 students.

"This one playlist had a lot of German techno," Aubrey said. "We predicted this was a kid wearing a mesh shirt who wanted to be a Nazi." At a party shortly afterward, Aubrey recognized the playlist and asked whose music it was. "They pointed to this kid in a mesh shirt with a swastika on his arm," Aubrey said. Students are starting to realize they must manage their music collections, or at least prune them, or risk permanently damaging their image, Aubrey said. He confessed to deleting a lot of stuff himself. "I had a lot of show tunes I had to get rid of," he said. "And a lot of punk pop from my earlier days, like Green Day and Blink-182."

There's a flip side, of course. If someone's music collection is not awful but actually pretty good, their social star can rise. Apparently, Tony "Father of the iPod" Fadell, who heads up Apple's iPod group, gets a lot of email from college kids thanking him for their improved sex lives, Mitch Ratcliffe, a Silicon Valley consultant, reported on his blog. According to Ratcliffe, Fadell told him over lunch that students with cool iTunes playlists can expect late-night visits from prospective lovers. "When they publish their playlists to Rendezvous networks in their dorms, other students surf those playlists to get an idea what people are like," Ratcliffe wrote. "So, late at night a guy sitting in his dorm may hear a knock on the door and, opening it, find a girl who loves their playlist. Tony gets mail from guys thanking him for this."

Sharing playlists can reveal quite a lot about someone's personal life too, as web developer Stefan Geens discovered. Geens lives in a Stockholm apartment block with about 100 residents who share the building's computer network. Thanks to the open network, Geens has access to his neighbors' iTunes libraries. The first thing he does when a new playlist pops up is Google the owner's name. "I have definitely learned things," Geens said. "I've got a film producer in my apartment, as well as a manager of a reasonably well known Stockholm band." The playlists can be even more revealing than what a Google  search turns up, Geens said. One neighbor has playlists of Swedish hip-hop labeled "Music for CD for XXX" and "XXX's sex songs." "I assume he doesn't care [that everyone else has access]," Geens said. Like his neighbors, Geens shares his music uncensored. "I am quite happy to advertise my music tastes," he said. "Music isn't porn, after all."

Music may not be porn, but it sometimes comes close. University of Maryland student Alexander Payne said that, while there's nothing in his collection considered shocking by his classmates, at home, it's a different matter. With family, there may be risks in letting it all hang out. "My PowerBook G4-toting mother was marveling at the Rendezvous feature when she saw 'Eat Shit You Fucking Redneck' by Pigface, 'Fuck the Pain Away' by Peaches, and so forth and arched a questioning eyebrow at me before moving on to my Django Reinhardt collection," Payne said. "All I could do was grin sheepishly."

AYLISTISM

Playlistism Evolves

John Zeratsky, a student at the University of Wisconsin, observed other students using shared playlists to send messages to one another. "iTunes sharing has become something of a cross between a bulletin board, software update notice, and file-sharing service," Zeratsky wrote on his blog. "Although it is only on a small scale, people are figuring out that they can communicate and connect through iTunes. I wouldn't be surprised if people start self-identifying themselves, like 'if you want to talk, IM me' or even 'I'm in the corner, wearing orange.'"

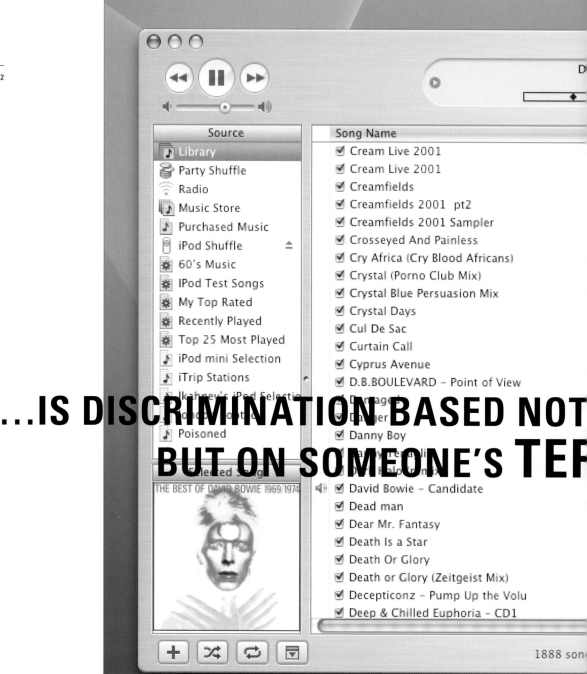

...IS DISCRIMINATION BASED NOT
BUT ON SOMEONE'S TER

iTunes users risk humiliation and "playlistism"
when they reveal their musical preferences across
open networks. But if the music's good, it can lead
to a hookup. CREDIT: APPLE COMPUTER

ON RACE, SEX, OR RELIGION,
RIBLE TASTE IN MUSIC…

HIDE YOUR iPOD, HERE COMES BILL

Microsoft's leafy corporate campus in Redmond, Washington, is beginning to look like the streets of New York, London, and just about everywhere else. Wherever you go, white headphones dangle from peoples' ears. To the growing frustration and annoyance of Microsoft's management, the iPod is wildly popular among Microsoft's workers. "About 80 percent of Microsoft employees who have a portable music player have an iPod," said one source, a high-level manager who asked to remain anonymous. "It's pretty staggering."

The source estimated that maybe 80 percent of Microsoft employees have a music player—80 percent of 80 percent translates to 16,000 iPod users among the 25,000 who work at or near Microsoft's corporate campus. "This irks the management team no end," said the source. The manager admitted his estimate might be high, but said it was based on the number of shared playlists that show up on the campus network, the chatter on internal mailing lists, and the number of white earbuds he's seen.

However, owning an iPod at Microsoft is beginning to become impolitic, so employees are hiding their iPods by swapping the telltale white headphones for a less conspicuous pair. "Some people are a bit concerned about being traitors, not supporting the company," he said. "They're a bit stealth about it."

How stealthy they must get varies from division to division. At the company's Macintosh Business Unit, which publishes a wide range of software for the Mac, owning an iPod is almost *de rigueur*. But at the Windows Digital Media Group, which is charged with making software for rival portable players, using an iPod is not a good career move. "In the media group they all smoke the company dope on that one," the manager said.

Of course, Microsoft's software is used by dozens of competing music players from manufacturers such as Creative Technology, Rio, and Sony. Its Windows Media Audio, or WMA, format is supported by several online music stores, including Napster, Musicmatch, and Wal-Mart. Microsoft's PlaysForSure program markets this choice as a boon for consumers. Nonetheless, in 2004, the iPod commanded 65 percent of the portable player market, and Apple's online iTunes Music Store 70 percent of online music sales, according to Apple.

"These guys are really quite scared," the anonymous source said of Microsoft's management. "It shows how their backs are against the wall.... Even though it's Microsoft, no one is interested in what we have to offer, even our own employees."

Mary Jo Foley, editor of Microsoft Watch, said she had no knowledge of the iPod's popularity on Microsoft's campus, but has noticed a lot of iPod chatter among Microsoft's legions of bloggers. "I have seen lots of Softies blog about it, though," she wrote in an email.

Microsoftie Chris Anderson, for example, just blogged about buying himself an iPod, three days after buying one for his wife. "I couldn't resist anymore," he wrote. "The industrial design on the iPod is absolutely amazing. The usability of the device is light-years beyond anything else I've seen."

Robert Scoble, who calls himself the "Microsoft Geek Blogger" and is one of the company's most widely read and vocal mouthpieces, said he knows lots of Microsoft employees with iPods. "I know many Microsoft employees who own iPods," he wrote on his blog in October 2004.

The unnamed Microsoft manager said he's heard from several executives who dutifully bought Microsoft-powered players, tried them, failed to get them working, and returned them in favor of an iPod. He went through the same experience, he said.

He had no idea if Bill Gates or Steve Ballmer, Microsoft's CEO, own iPods—he's never seen what gadgets they use. "I've never seen either of them with any device, but I only see them in meetings," he said.

So popular is the iPod, Microsoft executives are increasingly sending out memos frowning on its use. "There are frequent communications within the company about why it's a bad choice," the anonymous manager

Bill Gates and his iPod. **CREDIT**: PHOTOSHOP COLLAGE BY RYAN RAFFERTY

said. "So many people have chosen the iPod, executives feel they should send out memos about it." For example, an internal email sent to several senior managers in mid-December 2004 talked about iPod shipments to Apple's nearby store in Bellevue. The email said: "FWIW, the gal at the Bellevue Square Apple Store said that they are getting in two shipments of 200 iPods every day to keep up with this week's demand, and are nearly constantly selling out."

The note prompted a curt reply from Dave Fester, general manager of the Windows Digital Media division, who wrote the group: "I sure hope Microsoft employees are not buying iPods. We have great alternatives."

Fifteen minutes later, the person who wrote the initial email responded: "I don't know what I was thinking. I'm sure that Microsoft employees are not buying iPods, or Macs or PlayStations."

In 2003, Fester stirred up considerable controversy by criticizing Apple for locking in consumers with proprietary file formats, despite Microsoft's long history of using the same tactic.

As for hiding his own iPod use, the anonymous manager said he flaunts his iPod, despite the constant comments—and occasional arguments—it prompts. "I don't really care if it pisses them off," he said. "I'll argue why they're doing it wrong. If you want me to stop using it, give me a product that works and is as easy to use."

Neither Apple nor Microsoft responded to requests for comment.

iPod etiquette can be a tricky matter. When talking to a stranger, should you remove both earbuds or just one? What if it's your boss? According to Apple's guide to iPod etiquette, you should remove both earbuds if you're at a job interview, but only one when buying groceries. It's OK to keep both in when visiting in-laws.

How about copying music off someone else's iPod? (It's technically tricky, but doable.) The New York Metro's Help Desk advice column got a letter from someone saying he was uncomfortable sharing his music with a coworker. The Metro advised: "... admit that the idea of 'lending' out your hard-won collection makes you really uncomfortable. Then laugh nervously. Place your earplugs in your ears. And crank 'You Can't Always Get What You Want.'"

iPod Etiquette

U2: APPLE'S SAVING MUSIC FOR THE FUTURE

It's obvious that U2 are canny marketers and no strangers to the demands of commerce, but the band's endorsement of the iPod isn't just a simple cobranding deal. U2, with lead singer Bono as its charismatic spokesperson, are endorsing the whole idea of digital music. The band sincerely believes the future of music lies on the Internet, and, beyond just promoting iPods, they're championing the notion that the music industry should embrace the Net.

At the launch of the U2 iPod in San Jose in October 2004, Bono and guitarist The Edge joined Steve Jobs on stage. Jobs introduced the black special edition U2 iPod, which holds the entire U2 canon of 16 albums and more than 400 songs, as the world's first "digital boxed set." After playing a tune for the audience of journalists and music executives, The Edge said he was both "excited and appalled" by Napster, but online distribution clearly represented the future of music. "As long as we find a way to get paid, this ultimately would be a good thing," he said. "I see this as the beginning of a new era in the distribution of music. It's a good thing.... That's why we're here today, to be a little part of music history."

Bono chimed in that music labels were stuck in the past. He mocked executives who still called it the "record industry." "We haven't made records for years," Bono said.

In a 2004 *Irish Times* interview, the band said they've never allowed their music to be in TV commercials, but they did allow Apple to use the hit song "Vertigo" to advertise the iPod. Hypocritical? Not according to U2, who see themselves as supporting a cause as much as a company. "[Apple has] single-handedly saved the music industry," said drummer Larry Mullen. "They have developed the technology to download the music and for it to be paid for. Record companies couldn't do that. They were faffing around suing people.... Apple and Steve Jobs are saving music for the future. It won't be Universal, EMI, or Sony running record companies in 10 years' time—it will be Apple and telephone companies. We don't do advertisements; we did do the Apple campaign."

Bono said no money changed hands.

Jupiter analyst Joe Wilcox noted on his blog, "The music industry is about artists and fans' passion for bands like U2. I think the participation sends a message that bands like U2 back iTunes and iPod, which can extend their appeal."

Republican Rep. John Doolittle.
CREDIT: JOHN DOOLITTLE

Mr. iPod Goes to Washington

The humble iPod made Republican Rep. John Doolittle see the light on copyright fair use. Doolittle brandished an iPod in Congress while arguing for a relaxation of copyright restrictions in 1998's Digital Millennium Copyright Act. Under the act, copying music from one device to another — like an iPod — may be illegal.

"I paid for this," Doolittle said, waving the iPod before the packed hearing room, according to the *Sacramento Bee*. "I bought the material I want to record on it. But I may be prevented from taking advantage of this handy device." "I didn't grasp the issues before us in 1998," he continued. "We went way overboard. This needs to be corrected."

Also needing correction is Doolittle's taste in music: Andrew Lloyd Webber, ABBA, golden oldies, and foot-stomping country.

...THE iPOD ISN'T SIMPLY AN UPDATED WALKMAN. IT'S AN **ENTIRELY NEW BEAST**: A REVOLUTIONARY DEVICE THAT TRANSFORMS LISTENERS INTO "CYBORGS"...

MY iPOD, MY SELF

Markus Giesler has some colorful ideas about the iPod. He argues it transforms listeners into "cyborg consumers" and that it plugs them into a "hybrid entertainment matrix" where they can achieve "technotranscendence." Giesler is a 28-year-old assistant professor of marketing at York University in Toronto, and he is fast becoming a bright light in high-tech consumer research. A former record producer and label owner, Giesler has researched and written extensively on technology, consumption, and marketing. He has published papers on topics as varied as the gift economy of Napster, risk-taking in online file sharing, and "post-human consumer culture." In 2004, Giesler started studying iPod users and their music-listening habits. He set up the iPod Stories website to solicit tales of iPod consumption, which he plans to craft into an ethnographic study called "iPod Therefore iAm."

Russ Belk, a consumer behaviorist at the University of Utah, said Giesler is one of the best-recognized experts studying high-tech consumer behavior. "Perhaps it was his earlier success as a musician synthesizing jingles for advertising, but Markus has a way of seeing harmonies and disharmonies between people and technologies," said Belk.

According to Giesler's preliminary research, the iPod isn't simply an updated Walkman. It's an entirely new beast: a revolutionary device that transforms listeners into "cyborgs" through a process he calls "technotranscendence." Unlike the Walkman, the iPod taps into a "hybrid entertainment matrix," in which functions like random shuffle are a key construct, not just a convenient marketing hook.

"iPod and user form a cybernetic unit," said Giesler. "We're always talking about cyborgs in the context of cultural theory and sci-fi literature, but this is an excellent example that they're out there in the marketplace.... I have seen the future, and it is called the cyborg consumer." The cyborg consumer, Giesler said, is one who uses several technologies—from cell phones to Viagra—and is highly connected, both technically and socially. The iPod, for example, isn't just an MP3 player. It's an extension of the memory: storing the soundtrack of a lifetime, as well as names, addresses, calendars, and notes.

Giesler notes that users give their iPods names and carry them close to their bodies—the vibrations of the hard drive makes the device feel alive. "Consumers often say the iPod has become part of themselves," Giesler said. "The iPod is no longer just an instrument or a tool, but a part of myself. It's a body extension. It's part of my memory, and if I lose this stuff, I lose part of my identity."

Giesler argues that technological products such as the iPod allow consumers to become "technotranscendent." Consumers transcend the here and now through the use of technology, like kids playing video games. "They're not sitting in front of the TV; they're inside the game," said Giesler. "They have transcended their existence in front of the TV through the technology of the game."

Giesler said that the iPod plugs into a "hybrid entertainment matrix"—a complex network made in part of the iPod, a computer, the Internet, online music stores, file-sharing networks, and so on.

"The consumer is plugged into all kinds of technologies and networks that affect consumer behavior," he said. "As a result, consumption patterns change: from materiality to information—the Internet; from ownership to access—file sharing; and from pattern to randomness—the iPod."

Apple exemplifies this new paradigm with its troika of the iPod, the iTunes software that manages it, and the online store for buying new music. "Apple ... is selling a hybrid entertainment matrix—iPod, computer, and music store," Giesler said. "The iPod is important, but it's only really useful when it's interconnected. It becomes great when it is interconnected."

Giesler notes that jacking into the entertainment matrix changes consumption patterns. Random shuffle, for example, isn't just a novel way to listen to music; it's one of the key constructs of digital entertainment. Giesler said that instead of trading individual songs, users are starting to trade entire hard drives: giant libraries of music or movies. When interviewees are asked how they dip into these libraries, picking items at random is the most common answer. "Shuffle mode used to be a gimmick. Now it is the most viable strategy to access information that would otherwise be lost," he said. "It reduces the complexity of consumption. It's a cyborg consumption strategy."

Consumer researcher Markus Giesler argues that the iPod is leading the charge toward "cyborg consumerism," in which technology is married to the body and we plug into a vast "hybrid entertainment matrix." CREDIT: COURTESY OF JAN-PHILIPP BURGARD

iRAQ

Prominent ad campaigns have long been adapted or co-opted for political protest. As war raged in Iraq, the distinctive imagery of Apple's iPod campaign became the theme for a series of high-profile antiwar posters. A series of four posters depicting images from the war as stark silhouettes seemed to appear overnight in U.S. and European cities in the fall of 2004. One of the posters showed the notorious image of an Iraqi inmate at the infamous Abu Ghraib prison, where detainees were tortured and mistreated. The electrodes attached to the hooded prisoner's hands had been colored white to resemble the iPod's white earbuds. The poster reads "iRaq" and Apple's logo has been replaced with the image of a hand-grenade.

The posters were created anonymously by a pair of Los Angeles–based artists, who uploaded them to the Forkscrew Graphics website. The artists encouraged friends and activists to download the high-resolution images, print them, and post them. Since they closely resembled authentic advertising posters, they blended in seamlessly on city walls and construction barriers. "The iRaq poster project was created to remind the public that we are at war," said one of the artists, who asked to remain anonymous. "We simply used the language and iconography of an incredibly visible campaign to help stimulate dialogue surrounding what we feel is an incredibly important and complicated issue."

10,000 Iraqis killed. 773 US soldiers dead.

10,000 Iraqis killed. 773 US soldiers dead.

10,000 Iraqis killed. 773 US soldiers dead.

iPODHEADS

In newspapers and magazines, there's no shortage of pundits wringing their hands over how the iPod isolates listeners from their environment. The iPod is antisocial, they cry.

In the *Times*, British columnist Andrew Sullivan wrote: "Technology has given us a universe entirely for ourselves—where the serendipity of meeting a new stranger, hearing a piece of music we would never choose for ourselves or an opinion that might force us to change our mind about something are all effectively banished."

The *New York Times* complained, the iPod has transformed Manhattan into an island of "zombie-like robots...the only sign they are not quite human: two white wires that run from their ears into their clothes, just below the neckline, as distinctive as the bolts in the Frankenstein monster's neck."

In the London *Observer*, journalist John Naughton complained about the lack of communication between people on Britain's streets. "Imagine the future: a crowded urban street, filled not with people interacting with one another, but with atomised individuals cocooned in their personalised sound-bubbles, moving from one retail opportunity to another," he wrote.

But it's not the technology that makes people antisocial, it's culture. Jason Kottke, a blogger who lives in New York, argues that the car, the suburb, and the television are more antisocial than the Walkman or iPod. "Living in the suburbs and heavy automobile usage have made Americans unaccustomed to casual conversation with strangers...we're out of practice," he wrote. "Life moves a lot faster than it used to as well. We don't have time for casual conversations with strangers anymore; our time is reserved for working, sleeping, interacting with people we already know (family, coworkers, friends, the gang at the bar), and getting to and from places where we do those things as quickly as possible. The mobile phone, Sony Walkman, and iPod fit comfortably into that type of culture, but I don't think they're driving it."

The **Joy of Tech**™   by Nitrozac & Snaggy

©2005 Geek Culture®

joyoftech.com

INDEX

transmitters
    for antique radios, 96–97
    FM, 83, 109
    iTrip, 109
trends, 62
tube amps, 128–129
Turek, Dan, 17

U

U2 iPod, 14, 136–137
unveiling, iPod, 9–10
    iTunes introduction, 14
    reaction to, 10–13
    sales and changes, 13–14
USB 2
    added to iPod, 14
    key-chain drives, 79
    storage on, 76

V

vCard file format, 73
versatility, 5
video, 98–99
vinyl LPs, 3, 26
virtual iPod, 41
virtual shoplifters, 79
voter apologies, 83

W

Walkman sales, 13
war in Iraq, 140–142
weapons, iPods as, 13
Webb, Kevin, 78
white earbuds phenomenon, 18, 44–46, 62–64, 106
Wiesenthal, Lara, 110, 112
Wilcox, Joe, 110, 136
Windows-compatible versions, 73
Wipperfurth, Alex, 62
Wizard, 84
Wright, Jim, 76

Y

Yee, Philip, 80
Yi, Danny, 125, 127
Yoak, 82

Z

Zapp, Michael, 73
Zeratsky, John, 131

ABOUT THE AUTHOR

Leander Kahney is an editor at Wired News, where his Cult of Mac blog is a reader favorite. Previously, Kahney covered Apple and the Mac community for Wired News. He treats his subjects with insight and humor, and his experiences interacting with Mac fanatics and attending Mac events around the world are highly entertaining. Kahney's work introduces an element of warmth not usually associated with technology reporting.

LEANDER KAHNEY